Francis St. John Thackeray

Sermons Preached in Eton College Chapel 1870-1897

Francis St. John Thackeray

Sermons Preached in Eton College Chapel 1870-1897

ISBN/EAN: 9783744742993

Printed in Europe, USA, Canada, Australia, Japan

Cover: Foto ©Lupo / pixelio.de

More available books at **www.hansebooks.com**

SERMONS

PREACHED IN

ETON COLLEGE CHAPEL

1870—1897

BY

FRANCIS St. JOHN THACKERAY, M.A., F.S.A.

VICAR OF MAPLEDURHAM, FORMERLY FELLOW OF LINCOLN COLLEGE,
OXFORD, AND ASSISTANT MASTER AT ETON.

LONDON
GEORGE BELL AND SONS
1897

CONTENTS.

PAGE

SERMON I. *June 26th*, 1870.
Blessings forfeited through neglect (Isaiah v. 4). 1

SERMON II. *May 14th*, 1871.
The Great Alternative (John vi. 68) . . . 15

SERMON III. *November 26th*, 1871.
The Tyranny of Sin (Romans vi. 14) . . . 31

SERMON IV. Quinquagesima Sunday. *February 23rd*, 1873.
God's Final Revelation of Himself in Christ (Hebrews i. 1) 47

SERMON V. *May 18th*, 1873.
Permanence amidst Change (Psalm cii. 26, 27) . 61

SERMON VI. *November 9th*, 1873.
These three years (Luke xiii. 7) 76

SERMON VII. *February 28th*, 1875.
The Book of Job (Job xiii. 26) 90

SERMON VIII. *February 6th*, 1876.
Light Natural and Spiritual (Psalm xxxvi. 9) . 105

SERMON IX. *October 5th*, 1879.
The Regulation of Thoughts (Psalm cxxxix. 23). 120

SERMON X. *September 25th*, 1881.
The Misuse of Words: Perversion of Language (Isaiah xxxii. 5) 135

SERMON XI. *April 29th*, 1883.
The Recovery of Hezekiah (Isaiah xxxviii. 5) . 147

SERMON XII. *July 8th*, 1883.
A Farewell (John xxi. 21) 161

SERMON XIII. *June 19th*, 1892.
The Healing of the Demoniac Boy (Luke ix. 42) 178

SERMON XIV. *June 18th*, 1893.
God's Lamp never extinguished (1 Samuel iii. 3) 190

SERMON XV. Quinquagesima Sunday. *February 28th*, 1897.
The Value of Inequality (Matthew xxv. 29) . 202

Sermon I.

BLESSINGS FORFEITED THROUGH NEGLECT.[1]

"What could have been done more to my vineyard, that I have not done in it? Wherefore, when I looked that it should bring forth grapes, brought it forth wild grapes?"—*Isaiah*, v. 4.

THE vine (it has often been remarked) furnished the inspired writers with a ready and appropriate metaphor. It is employed by them sometimes as a type of plenty and a symbol of prosperity; at other times, in a more restricted sense, as an emblem of the Hebrew polity and the Jewish Church. Nor can this surprise us, when we reflect upon the numerous properties for which it is conspicuous. The exuberant fertility of the vine, its quickness of growth, the great age to which it has been known to live, the degree in which the temperate enjoyment of its fruits

[1] June 26th, 1870.

promotes man's comfort — above. all, the watchful and incessant care which it demands as the price of its full benefits—all combine to point it out as a singularly prompt and expressive illustration of the blessings of Providence, blessings bestowed, indeed, with a large and bountiful hand, but still not lavished unconditionally, or so as to dispense with the need of labour on the part of the recipient; not shared equally by the careless and the diligent, but ever increasing in value, in proportion both to the use to which they are applied, and to the degree of cultivation with which we foster them.

I need not dwell upon the familiar instances of this figure, such as the Psalmist's [1] appeal to God to look down and visit the vine which he had brought out of Egypt; it recurs again and again in the Prophets;[2] and our text can hardly have failed to arrest our attention, as well from the intrinsic beauty of the passage as from the resemblance which it bears, in its general structure, to our Saviour's parable of the wicked husbandman. But while there is much that is common to both, they are not identical. The transfer of the vineyard to others has no counterpart in the Hebrew prophet. The central idea of the one is the trans-

[1] Ps. lxxx. 8-16.
[2] *E.g.*, Hos. x. 1; Jer. ii. 21; Ez. xix. 10.

fer of the vineyard from its first possessors through their own misconduct. The central idea in the Hebrew prophet is the Jewish nation and Church: "The vineyard of the Lord of Hosts is the house of Israel, and the men of Judah his pleasant plant."

Now, if we study the history of this extraordinary people—if we weigh well the causes and the consequences of *their* failure—we shall find that their fortunes are not something unconnected with ourselves, but that like causes will produce like effects, and the words of Isaiah, through the same Holy Spirit which dictated their original utterance, may become instinct with new force and life to each one of us present here this day.

Let us try to realize the circumstances which suggested them. The chapter where they occur stands by itself, and is directed against the growing corruptions of the nation, its warnings being probably called forth by the closing events of the reign of Jotham.

It was a time of material prosperity. Never since the separation of the northern kingdom had Judah reached such a height as she did under the auspices of Jotham and his father Uzziah. The latter had recovered from the Edomites the port of Elath on the Red Sea, had succeeded in reducing the outlying tribes, had organized a standing army, and fortified the capital with improved military engines. Nor had he paid less attention to the arts of peace. At home and abroad he had raised the position of his subjects. These advantages were maintained and even extended under the prudent reign of his son Jotham. But, again (as is too frequently the result of great material prosperity), it was a time of careless ease, of that overbearing pride and insolence, in which we so often recognize the parent of tyranny, and the forerunner of inevitable ruin. The growing affluence of the times had moved the Hebrew commonwealth farther and farther away from its original constitution. A commercial spirit had by degrees succeeded to the simplicity of earlier days. Gold and silver, introduced in abundance by the traffic lately reopened with the East, had brought in their train a love of effeminate delicacies, often stigmatized by the Prophets. Hence the six woes denounced in this fifth chapter of Isaiah against covetousness, riotous feasting, and reckless defiance of holy things ; against the misguided conscience which comes at last to call evil good, and good evil ; against the infatuated blindness of all who are "wise in their own eyes, and prudent in their own sight;" and, lastly, against those who perverted the administration of law for bribes. Jehovah looked for righteousness but beheld oppression. Well might the Lord of the Vineyard expostulate with it for its unfruitfulness: "What could have been done more to my vineyard, that I have not done in it? Wherefore, when I looked that it should bring forth grapes, brought it forth *poisonous berries?*" For such is the sense of the term wild grapes. No mere unprofitableness, but what is positively noxious and pernicious is signified. As by the tares in S. Matthew, not a different kind of seed, but a degenerate wheat, so here a degenerate grape is intended.

The tree once so fair—a vine of Sorek,[1] that is, the type of excellence in its class—has deteriorated from its primal perfection. And yet what more could have been done for God's own people in preparing the soil to be the depository of revealed truth? The vineyard was already fenced in by the geographical[2] peculiarities of Palestine. The remarkable cleft of the deep valley of the Jordan, the coast line with its scanty harbourage, the desert on the south, and the ranges of Lebanon on the north, formed each so many natural barriers. Nor were they less clearly marked out by the Mosaic law, with its distinctive

---

[1] Jer. ii. 21, ἄμπελον καρποφόρον πᾶσαν ἀληθινήν. Cf. John, xv. 1, ἐγώ εἰμι ἡ ἄμπελος ἡ ἀληθινή, "the true, the ideal vine."—WESTCOTT.

[2] Cf. Stanley, "Sinai and Palestine," pt. ii., ch. ii.

institutions, as destined to "dwell alone, and not to be reckoned among the nations."

And then, what could have been done more for the *development* of the Jewish race? Their whole history points to the gradual recovery of the knowledge of God, and the appearance of a Redeemer as the thread which binds together its several parts. We see a separation going on of families and tribes, whence there was the best hope of moral influence. There is a unity in the successive yearnings, aspirations, and promises—which become gradually more and more explicit, until an image appears with sufficient distinctness of a Being—Divine, yet Human—in whom is centred the restoration of man's lapsed and corrupted powers. In the life and teaching of Jesus Christ this wonderful history culminates.

And yet we know, in spite of all these precautions and advantages, selected as they were, and isolated from their neighbours, sheltered by their law, and honoured with special favours and miracles, how signally they failed. Nations have their time of trial, after which their doom is sealed. The piety of Hezekiah, the reforms of Josiah, could not avert the ruin which Isaiah saw to be impending. The Captivity, indeed, did much (as the discipline of sorrow will often do much) to purify the heart.

Among its lasting results were a keener sense of the evil of sin, and the value of prayer; a deeper insight into the sacrifice of the heart and will; a more enlightened belief as to the future life; above all, the old taint of idolatry was banished, never to return. But neither the Captivity, nor the humiliations of later years, when Judah had entered on a new career, could break their innate pride, or teach them to recognize their Messiah when they saw Him.

We know the sequel—the literal fulfilment of Christ's words—"the trench cast around them," the capital destroyed, the Temple polluted and demolished, the political existence of the people wiped out for ever. The horrors of that siege forms one of the blackest pages in history. "Jerusalem itself," it has been said, "has probably witnessed a far greater portion of human misery than any other spot upon the earth."[1]

And of the fortunes of this devoted race through succeeding ages (which have been vividly described by an historian whose boyhood was spent in this place) who is ignorant? at least of the general outline, if he be not familiar with the details of that melancholy picture? We have the extraordinary spectacle

---

[1] Milman, "History of the Jews," vol. ii., bk. xvi.

of a people brought, on several occasions, to the brink of extermination. We have a series of exactions and persecutions, often no doubt wantonly and cruelly inflicted, but often, too, the result of their own turbulence.

> "Lost branches of the once-lov'd vine,
>   Now wither'd, spent, and sere,
> See Israel's sons, like glowing brands,
> Tost wildly o'er a thousand lands,
> For twice a thousand year."[1]

One bright spot in the gloom of the Middle Ages stands out; one oasis in the desert of their woes. In Spain, from the tenth to the fifteenth century, the Jews not only lived unmolested in their traffic, but enjoyed prosperity as financiers, as physicians, and confidential ministers at the courts of kings. This was also the noonday of their literature, when schools of theology sprang up at Seville, at Cordova, and the other great cities of the south. The spirit of the Hebrew poetry was then, too, revived, and their harp reawoke an echo of its earlier music, even in a strange land. But this Golden Age was succeeded by an Iron Age, when the daylight set in utter darkness. And there are few scenes more touching than that in which we see the exiles forced to quit those smiling provinces which their com-

[1] The Christian Year, fifth Sunday in Lent.

merce, their industry, and their superior intelligence had done so much to improve.[1]

And now, if we pass from the history of the chosen race to the inner history of our personal lives,—may not the words of our text afford matter for grave and earnest reflection for each one of us?

"What could have been done more to my vineyard?" What (may it not be said without irreverence) could the Creator in the beginning have done more when he framed our nature? He made man a little lower than the angels, to crown him with that glorious prerogative of his nature, the power to choose the evil or the good,

"Sufficient to have stood, though free to fall."

Had it been otherwise, had man been placed outside the pale of possible danger, and been denied the mysterious gift of an individual free will, with all the honour and peril it entails, would he not have been a mere *automaton*, capable indeed of mechanically going through a dull routine of prescribed action, but utterly incapable of any ardent affection for a heavenly Father, of any allegiance to a Divine Master, of any lofty aspiration after the unseen and eternal?

[1] Milman, "History of the Jews," vol. iii., bk. xxvi.

What, again, could have been done more than has been done in the stupendous scheme of salvation, God the Father sending us a perfect pattern of a faultless life, and of self-sacrifice in his dear Son,—who loved us and gave Himself for us,—God the ever-blessed Comforter pleading for us, convincing us of sin,—and guiding us into all truth? And shall we then leave any portion of our hearts, any moment of our existence unconsecrated to Him?—For what could have been done more for each of us *here?* Each must acknowledge that he has received countless mercies, opportunities, it is to be feared, too often slighted, talents too often left to rust and moulder unused.

Will you not remember that you each have your vineyard to tend, your garden to cultivate? Will you allow it to run to waste, and become choked with unsightly weeds? Will you not look well that there be in it no branch with useless tendrils requiring to be lopped off, no poisonous berries of any one noxious habit.

In the varied life of this favoured spot, inheriting as it does a rich treasure of memories from the past, and continually engrafting on the past fresh improvements demanded by the wider scope and requirements of the present, — none can excuse themselves for standing idle instead of going into the vineyard, on the plea that he has no field for his energies. None can say that he does not find here an adequate sphere for his individual genius: none can fairly complain that his own special pursuit is passed by unrecognized and unrewarded. And if misgivings arise in the minds of any of us as to unfruitfulness, and if we question ourselves WHEREFORE when God looks for grapes, the vintage is so disproportionate to the care and culture and advantages we have received—shall we not find one great reason for this to lie in ourselves? The rank weeds grow up and the wild berries swell because we do not look within, and because we are so easily satisfied. Self-complacency is ever a source of stagnation, whether moral or intellectual. When that great restorer of Philosophy,—Lord Bacon, —in his masterly survey of human knowledge, passed in review the systems that had existed before his day, and asked why they had produced so little, he laid great stress upon the *complacency* with which men had regarded those feeble results, as not the least among the impediments by which science had been retarded. The idea of plenty (he says) was one of the causes of want.[1] The

---

[1] "Opinio copiæ inter causas inopiæ est."—*De Augmentis Scientiarum* (lib. ii.).

words are no less true of the laws which regulate spiritual growth, than they were of the search into the laws of Nature. Does not the propensity to believe that we have "already attained," that "we are rich and have need of nothing"—lie at the root of more than half our failures? Can we not often trace deterioration to our making light of such helps as prayer, and dismissing them at once without a trial? A few moments' quiet withdrawal from the world, a few verses of the New Testament allowed to lodge daily in the mind and the memory, may protect the defences of your vineyard past all belief, may guard it from being broken in upon and spoiled by the evil one.

Moral thoughtfulness and sober mindedness, a due distrust of self, a timely dread of lethargy, these are among the qualities we desire when we pray (as Christ bids us do) for labourers for His harvest, and reinforcements for His army. Yes! here His work may and must be furthered by you. There is ground untilled at our doors, and the modes of culture are manifold. Not by one channel does the Holy Spirit reach you. Not into any one groove or type would true wisdom force the ardent energies of youth. The stronger character, who will use the influence which he possesses over his friend for good and not for evil; the scrupulous adherent to truthfulness, who will not circulate groundless reports or damaging slander; the merciful and considerate boy, who will not by harsh act, or perhaps harsher word, needlessly pain his more sensitive companion; the guileless spirit that will not suffer itself to be entangled in the web of current fallacies and pernicious school traditions; the patient student, steadily advancing from strength to strength; the young man, who, in the full enjoyment of physical strength—while he thanks God for the glow of health and the consciousness of vigour which animates his frame—yet remembers that he must give account for all this—who, if the Saviour Himself with earnest, searching gaze bent on him, were to ask him, "*Lovest thou me more than these?*"—these amusements of a day—could answer from his heart, "*Yea, Lord, thou knowest that I love thee,*" —all these, and such as these, are doing good work in their Master's vineyard. Their tree will blossom and fructify in due season. Let them take comfort and go on. Whatsoever their hand findeth to do, let them do it with their might. Only let them not rely on self. Let them listen to Christ, who tells us that the sole source of goodness is in Himself, as the boughs derive quickening life only from the sap that is sent them from the root and from the stem.

"Abide in me, and I in you. As the branch cannot bear fruit of itself, except it abide in the vine; no more can ye, except ye abide in me. I am the vine, ye are the branches: he that abideth in me, and I in him, the same bringeth forth much fruit: for without me ye can do nothing."

Sermon II.

THE GREAT ALTERNATIVE.[1]

"Then Simon Peter answered him, Lord, to whom shall we go? thou hast the words of eternal life."— *St. John*, vi. 68.

THESE words remind us of a sad and startling defection. The chapter at the close of which they occur, contains one of those touches of reality by which the Gospel is throughout stamped, even where we least look for it. In describing the rise of any other society, it would not have been thought necessary to mention the apparent failures that obstructed it in its earlier stages. But the Evangelists are too deeply penetrated with the truth of their message, too completely convinced of its sacred origin, to keep back any circumstance, because at the first glance it might seem to indicate imperfection. There is no attempt to tone down or suppress what might make against their cause. As St. Matthew tells us that our Lord did not many miracles among his own countrymen,

[1] May 14th, 1871.

"because of their unbelief," as St. Luke frankly admits of Paul's first preaching at Rome, that while "some believed the things that were spoken, *some believed them not*," so the passage before us refers to that critical period when "many went back and walked no more with Christ." The air of reality, the simplicity, the candour with which such statements are made, has been pointed out[1] as one link in the chain of evidence to its truth which Christianity furnishes out of its own records.

And undoubtedly that divine discourse which St. John adds to the account of the miraculous feeding of the 5,000, must have been full of difficulty to those who received it in a hostile and carping spirit. It would naturally rouse opposition when taken in its bare and literal sense. We find, accordingly, that the very same men, who, while impressed by a momentary awe, had wished to come and take Jesus by force and make Him a king, who had followed Him across the Galilæan Lake, and gone so far in their professions of attachment as to ask what works they should do that they might work the works of God—we find that these same men refused to hear him any longer when He

---

[1] Paley, "Evidences of Christianity," pt. ii., ch. iii.

began to unfold the inner significance of that supernatural act which they had witnessed on the previous day.

Scarcely does He begin when they demand a sign, as though none had been already given. They murmur because He says, "I am the bread which came down from heaven." They strive among themselves. "How *can* this man give us his flesh to eat?"

And not they alone were offended. Even to the more immediate group of the disciples the words were scarcely less hard. Neither did His brethren, His own kindred, bound to him by ties of earthly relationship, neither did they at this time believe in Him. And Christ could foresee a yet greater loneliness. The very words that reveal the fount of strength within Him, "I am not alone, because the Father is with me," how much do they at the same time suggest of isolation from those around Him! Consider what that isolation must have been. Imagine what it is to the founder of even a human brotherhood to be gradually deserted by the inner circle of trusted friends; what a sharp pang must be felt as, one after another, followers are estranged and alienated; when coldness takes the place of attachment, and apathy, if not professed dislike, succeeds to ardent and enthusiastic devotion. Think of Elijah, left to stem the torrent of idolatry, when, from the solitude of Horeb, he cries out in despairing accents, "I have been very jealous for the Lord God of hosts, for I, even I only am left, and they seek my life to take it away." Think of Athanasius, four times an exile, bearing witness in his single person to the Faith, so that *Athanasius contra mundum* was scarcely an exaggeration of the truth.

Still all such instances of desertion are but the faintest and feeblest images of Christ's loneliness. In the first place He only could know all the peril that this rejection of Him involved. None other without the grossest blasphemy could say, *I am the Light of the world.* None else, therefore, could fathom the abyss of darkness which remained for those who wilfully shut their eyes against it.

And secondly, from the perfection of His human nature, his sense of isolation must have been unparalleled. For His affections, and the sensibilities of that nature were such, in their keenness and intensity, as we can but dimly conceive. Infinitely more, therefore, than we experience when the ties of the closest friendship or the warmest allegiance are snapped, must He have felt as His friends fell off from His side.

Then it was, when the defection even of the Apostles seemed imminent, that in answer to this sorrowful inquiry, "*Will ye also go away?*" Peter's deeply suggestive question was put, "*Lord, to whom shall we go?*" Let us consider the question more particularly —and the answer—so like his celebrated confession, "Thou art the Christ, the Son of the living God," which that loving, impulsive, earnest character spontaneously supplied— "THOU hast the words of eternal life."

To whom could they go? To the cramped and shallow system of Judaism, overlaid by the glosses and perversions of its false exponents? Surely not to those "weak and beggarly elements" could they again return? Illiterate and unpractised men, as they were, what comfort or support in their daily life, what hope for the future, what solution of their difficulties, what enlightenment in their ignorance could they discern amid the clouds and mists in which the teachers of the day had wrapped the truth? those blind leaders of the blind, who had taken away the key of knowledge, entering not in themselves, and hindering those who were anxious to enter in? Should they go to the Pharisees? whose hypocrisy they had seen unmasked, who would help an ox out of a pit, but not a human sufferer out of his infirmity on the Sabbath, and whose distorted teaching was powerless to lift a soul out of the mire of sin.

Surely after what they had seen it was not from such that they could expect guidance. After hearing the voice that hushed the angry elements, breathed vigour into the Centurion's servant, and forgiveness to the restored paralytic, none other could satisfy their longings. After having seen the glory of the Son, full of grace and truth, could they go back to prophet, priest, or lawgiver? After gazing on the substance, could they rest content with the shadow or the type?

And if we now enlarge the horizon of our view beyond the limits of the Holy Land, if we regard the question "To whom shall we go?" as coming from the human race at the time of Christ's advent, what hope of deliverance was elsewhere to be found? The empire of Rome, with all its network of civilization, its magnificent roads, its system of jurisprudence, its rich inheritance of material and intellectual wealth, was corrupt at the core. Fair and dazzling as the surface might be, the malady was deeply seated, and was, in truth, ineradicable save by divine agency.

We have but to remember the dark picture drawn in the first chapter of the Epistle to the Romans, the mass of accumulated sins, which age after age the troubled waters of heathendom had thrown up. Forgetfulness of the Creator led to pride; pride (as it will ever do) brought with it ignorance, and from ignorance resulted the most frightful rebellion against God and Nature, until God also gave man over to a reprobate mind.

And yet in this continuous declension, in this onward tide of wickedness, to which each generation contributed its share, there must have been many an earnest spirit that strove to resist the current. Many a simple uneducated Greek or Roman, like the Centurion of Capernaum, or the jailor at Philippi, must have longed to break the bondage of society, under which he bowed, and to disentangle himself, even were it mortal agony to do so, from the poisoned robe of evil habits, which was clinging round and eating into his soul. Many a sincere thinker, again, *did* contend patiently for truth and certainty upon the great subjects of Virtue and Happiness, Death, Judgment, and Immortality.

But each of these classes, the learned and the unlearned alike, must have confessed the nothingness of unaided human effort; each must have felt a void that could only be filled by the authoritative "words of eternal life." From each must the thought have again and again been wrung, "*To whom shall we go?*"

For consider their *religious life*[1] in some of

---

[1] Cf. Döllinger, "The Gentile and the Jew in the Courts of the Temple of Christ," bks. ii. and iii., by

its aspects. The popular worship, with all its elaborate pomp and "palpable array of sense," had nothing to offer to the deepest instincts of mankind. It did not even pretend to smooth the path of daily life. It was addressed to the fancy, not to the conscience. As to who or what the Supreme Being was the ordinary pagan had but a confused notion. And this perplexity increased as successive additions were made to the national cult, both by the creative imagination of the Greek, and the free importation of foreign deities. The deification of the powers of Nature, and the assigning to each element and spot its tutelary god, opened out a boundless field for invention. The next step was to subject them to the conditions of time and space, and clothe them with the passions and infirmities of men. The stream could not rise higher than its source; and though a few might grasp a more elevated belief in a Providence, and see how it conflicted with the degrading legends of mythology, to the bulk of mankind the objects of their worship were removed from themselves only in degree.

But religion was woven into their whole public and private existence. True: there were the *externals* of ritual and ceremony.

which much of this and the following paragraphs were suggested.

There were the oracles, which for a time at least *were* perhaps overruled for good. There were prescribed formulæ of prayer, solemn sacrifices, temples, and a priesthood. But no religious instruction was expected from the priests, no life-giving words issued from the temples, and the prayers and sacrifices (if we except a few occasional expressions in the poets) were prompted by nothing higher than a hope of winning some material benefits, or appeasing the divine jealousy, or at best were a thanksgiving for past protection. There remained the purifications and the *mysteries*, particularly those of Eleusis, which some have regarded as the best and noblest feature in the religion of the Greeks. Is it to be supposed for a moment that these wrought any lasting change in the spectators? The promise was indeed held out that the future of the initiated would be more favoured than that of others, but this advantage was not forfeited by subsequent transgression. They did not counteract the errors of the popular creed. They were simply a dramatic representation of legends, in which deceit and imposture rather than any lessons of purity predominated. In truth, the idea of purification as a moral rather than a physical cleansing, apart from a few isolated passages, is foreign to the whole range of heathen thought.

So feeble then was the reed upon which the heathen had to rely in his *Religion*. Should he go to *Philosophy*, and would he fare better at her hands? Here at least, amid the comfortless views of life which met anxious seekers after God, some peace of mind, some firm basis of teaching might be anticipated. For Philosophy was not without reason, called by Clement of Alexandria a gift entrusted by Providence to the best of the Greeks, as an education for Christianity.[1] How far it was this, is of course much too large a subject for a sermon: we can only speak, and that very briefly, of its most brilliant representative, Plato.

That rare and gifted intellect, whose writings for seven centuries exercised a profound influence upon human thought, had set before himself the noblest of ends:—to clear away the false notions engendered by the state religion; to liberate the mind from error; and to direct it upwards to the Future, the Invisible, the Eternal.

And had his system (pruned of some extravagances) attained sufficient mastery and scope, it would perhaps have done more than anything else short of Revelation to regenerate ancient society. He could grasp the idea of

---

[1] Clem. Alex. Strom., vi. 693, 694.

the one supreme good (though he confessed that his essence was unfathomable), by approximating to whom, as far as possible,[1] man could alone escape from the evil around him and in him.

Into this degenerate condition he held that we had lapsed by some primitive fall, whence our powers for virtue were greatly enfeebled, and the present life (he taught) contained the germ, and decided the complexion for happiness or misery of a future life. He could reason on the same truths which made Felix tremble "on righteousness, temperance, and a judgment to come." But (and here we see the limits of mere human speculations), he could not go on to declare that this judgment should be by a *man*, by Jesus, who was yet the Eternal Son of God, who was to live and die for us; touched with the feeling of our infirmities, but not tainted with our guilt.

Much as Platonism stimulated man's higher affections, and brought them to a clearer consciousness of their wants, we may trace at least *three* serious defects under which it laboured. It could contribute nothing to the knowledge of God as a Person. It raised the mind towards Goodness in the abstract, rather than towards the perfectly Good Being. And secondly,

---

[1] πειρᾶσθαι χρὴ ἐνθένδε ἐκεῖσε φεύγειν ὅ τι τάχιστα. φυγὴ δὲ ὁμοίωσις θεῷ κατὰ τὸ δυνατόν.—*Theætetus*, 176. A.

it shared the common error of heathen sentiment in failing to apprehend the deadly nature of Sin. Moral evil was in general estimated far too lightly by the Greeks, whose language scarcely discriminated between what was in itself sinful, and what was repulsive to the sense of beauty. Sin with Plato was a defect of intellectual insight, affecting a part only of our nature, instead of being the ruin of the whole man. Thus, then, as wisdom was the one universal virtue, ignorance the one deadly disease, and as none (he held) could *know* what was good without recognizing it as good, and instantly practising it,—therefore the soul had but to be brought face to face with the heavenly ideas, in order to accomplish its redemption.

And this shows us the third cardinal error of his system. The redemption which it held out was not *universal*. It was confined to but a few, to that small section of mankind which could scale the heights of Philosophy.

How wide a gulf separates this from the offer of Christ! "Come unto me *all* ye that labour and are heavy laden and I will give you rest." The gospel is likened to a net cast into the sea, that gathered of *every* kind. It claims every region of man's being, it embraces every diversity of character; the active life of devotion to others, no less than the life of contemplation, and the search after truth. It is the common heritage of the weak and of the strong, the rich and the poor, of the highest and of the lowest in the scale of culture and civilization. *All* must ask themselves, as the most vital of questions, *Lord, to whom shall we go?* all must echo the response, "Thou hast the words of eternal life." *The words of Christ!* Oh that you would store them up, as an antidote against the poison of evil! Study the Sermon on the Mount, the treasures contained in the Parables, the depth of love in the fourteenth and following chapters of St. John. Many noble and beautiful and spirit-stirring utterances we owe to the sages and poets of old. But they possess no healing power. They convey no message of pardon as Christ could. For He is the true Λόγος, the Revealer of God's love and mercy; the solver of the doubts that so long had tormented the human mind. "*The words of the Lord are pure words.*" In their light you will see light. Ask yourselves if His Blessing is indeed resting on your life; as it must rest, believe me, for any real happiness; as it will do, if there be not any root of bitterness—the total absence of zeal for goodness, the cold indifference about those who are struggling after holiness.

When you are tottering on the brink of actual wrong-doing—when you recall some act of which you now are ashamed, or when your life is steeped in some sudden sorrow or loss—oh! *to whom then shall you go?* Surely to Him, who knows you through and through, who has watched over you all these years, who will cleanse every guilt save that which scorns to be forgiven. Again, *The words of the Lord are authoritative, convincing words.* We instinctively feel that there is no appeal from them. "They were astonished" (we read) "at his doctrine, for his word was with power."

But, thirdly, there is not only the greatest majesty and authority in Christ's words. There is also the greatest *tenderness*. "All bare him witness and wondered at the gracious words which proceeded out of his mouth." "Peace I leave with you—my peace I give unto you." Or again, "Father, forgive them, for they know not what they do." He could sympathize with ordinary man, as none other could, while he hates the sin as perfect Goodness must everlastingly hate it. And often words of wholesome warning follow close upon acts of mercy: "Behold, thou art made whole" (he says to the man whom he had healed), "*sin no more, lest a worse thing come unto thee.*"

Once more, too, the words of Jesus Christ are the exact reflex and mirror of His life. "I am come not to do my own will, but the will of him that sent me." "Not as I will, but as thou wilt." Think of this, and when angry thoughts throng upon you, will you not recall His meekness, "who, when he was reviled, reviled not again?" Pray for a portion of that spirit of self-sacrifice! Be ashamed of many an idle word, of many a disingenuous evasion! Oh how mournfully will they rise up again to the memory in the day when they are viewed in immediate contrast with the image of death, and the solemnity of the life to come!

Well do we pray in the Litany, "From contempt OF THY WORD and Commandment, good Lord deliver us." "Heaven and earth," Christ said, "shall pass away, but my words shall not pass away." Yes! the heavens may "depart as a scroll that is rolled together;" the solid earth may witness a still mightier revolution than those vast gradual changes which geology tells us she has already undergone; but Christ's words "no time, no change can falsify." In the new heavens and new earth *they* shall still be heard, and willing or loth we must all listen to them. Why then reject them now? It surely cannot be from indifference to them: for they are " the words of eternal life." And no human being ever yet really longed for death.

> " 'Tis life whereof our nerves are scant,
> Oh life, not death, for which we pant;
> More life and fuller that I want."

Such, I am convinced, is the faithful expression of the aspirations of all who hear me. It must be then that we shrink from those sterner sayings which we feel condemn us. But we dare not dissever the compassionate tenderness of Christ from his wholesome and truthful severity. And, if our heart condemn us, still the question returns upon us "*to whom shall we go?*" Remember, "God is greater than our heart, and knoweth all things." Remember Christ's promise, "him that cometh unto me will I in no wise cast out."[1]

---

[1] In connection with the subject of this sermon the following passage from the conclusion of Milman's "History of Latin Christianity" may be here quoted:

"As it is my own confident belief that the words of Christ, and his words alone (the primal, indefeasible truths of Christianity), shall not pass away; so I cannot presume to say that men may not attain to a clearer, at the same time more full, comprehensive, and balanced sense of those words, than has as yet been generally received in the Christian world. As all else is transient and mutable, these only eternal and universal, assuredly, whatever light may be thrown on the mental constitution of man, even on the constitution of nature, and the laws which govern the world, will be concentered so as to give a more penetrating vision of those undying truths."

SERMON III.

THE TYRANNY OF SIN.

"Sin shall not have dominion over you: for ye are not under the law, but under grace."—*Romans*, vi. 14.

NONE but an inspired writer would have ventured upon such an assertion. For it must have seemed to be contradicted, at first sight, by daily and hourly experience. What a blest assurance, what a sustaining thought, what a real gospel for those to whom it was sent! May we not say that this was indeed one of those spiritual gifts, which at the opening of the epistle St. Paul says he longed to impart to the Roman converts whom as yet he had not seen?

How much do these few words contain! There is the great truth of gratuitous salvation through faith in Christ. And secondly, the announcement of *freedom*, freedom to the Jews from the oppressive weight of ordinances, which they could never hope to observe in each particular; freedom to the heathen from the galling fetters of the society in which he lived; freedom in the highest sense to the despised and neglected slave.

And yet how hard for those to whom it was sent to realize the message in all its depth! For consider what *was* the moral atmosphere breathed by a resident in Rome in the middle of the first century of our era.

It is easy, indeed, to draw an exaggerated contrast between the old and new world, and to dwell too exclusively on the depravity of Pagan life. There is a twofold danger in this. There is the danger of forgetting our own far heavier responsibilities and the danger of unduly depreciating the virtues which ancient civilization did undoubtedly produce and foster. Loyalty to the state, self-surrender for the public good, respect for the august majesty of law, manly courage, and dignity or gravity, to use his own favourite word, were—you will readily remember—the characteristic qualities of the Roman, at least during the earlier stages of his history. And we may admit that so far as these virtues had not wholly degenerated under foreign influences, so far there was much on which the higher teaching of Christianity would hope to build.

We may admit that, even under the Empire, there were some bright examples (such as Agricola and Thrasea) of guilelessness and unsullied faithfulness in the discharge of duty, to redeem the darker features of the age. Still after all honour is done to such names, whether in the camp or the senate, in philosophy or in private life, we must confess that Rome at this time was a most uncongenial soil for the development of the Christian graces. Uncongenial, truly, to human eyes; but God seeth not as man seeth. The wealthy voluptuaries, sated with the enervating indulgences of the bath, the banquet, and the circus, united softness of living with a callous insensibility to suffering in others. There could have been little cordiality among those troops of visitors who each morning thronged the vestibule of their patron; little feeling of home attachment among those crowds of slaves whom their lords scarcely recognized by sight. The poorer classes, on the other hand, with their appetite for amusement stimulated and gratified to excess, were unnaturally hardened by the constant spectacle of death exhibited in the amphitheatre.

And lastly, though freedom of discussion was permitted, it could not cure the mental and moral diseases of the more thoughtful who withdrew themselves from such corrupting influences. Stoicism was, perhaps, the best resource for the unaided intellect of the time: but Stoicism could promise no real comfort amidst the business of life. It rather counselled retirement from its temptations. It became, as has been said, "a consolation for inactivity, rather than a stimulus to action."

Such were some aspects of life in Rome when St. Paul wrote his Epistle. The first five years of Nero's reign, "the torrent's stillness ere it dash below"—from the external tranquility of which men fondly augured so well for the remainder—were now drawing to a close, when the enormities by which it will ever be remembered were to commence. And yet it was in a capital like this that St. Paul could find a noble sphere for the work of an Evangelizer. It was to the faithful few, almost lost in the vast mass of the heathen population,—to some servants in princely households, some freedmen, some soldiers in the prætorian barracks, witnesses of so much misery and so much guilt as they must have been, that he could say confidently, "*Sin shall not have dominion over you.*" The term he uses, "Sin shall not *lord it over you*," is a remarkable one. Originally it denoted an authority that owns limitation, and is exercised for the good of its subjects, as opposed to despotic unrestricted power. But it passes on to this latter signification, so that the two terms are frequently interchanged.

And is such language, dear brethren, too strong to express the final dominion, or rather domination of Sin? Alas! Those who have ever felt, if only for a time, the enthralling power of any one over-mastering passion,—how imperiously it carries everything before it,—will bear witness to its truth. The ungovernable spirit which will brook no thwarting, the force of appetites clamouring for instant gratification, the indulgence of lawless and rebellious thoughts, the unchecked utterance of hasty words,—these are facts too common not to warrant the assertion that sin can, and often does, exercise a fearful sway over man's nature: that it can mar the harmony and destroy the balance which should subsist between the different parts of which it is so wonderfully composed.

"Boundless intemperance in nature is a tyranny." And yet the subject of this tyranny is often the last to be aware of his condition. He would resent the name of slave. Does he not act exactly as he wishes? Yes, as his wishes and impulses prompt him, perhaps, but not as his will, his moral choice, his better judgment, direct. Thus the extremes of weakness and violence meet. You recollect the double use of the Latin word *impotens*, signifying first, weakness, then violence, and lastly, that union of passion with feebleness which is the precise state of one, who in fancied strength is really under the control of whatever appetite is uppermost.

How vivid an image of the thorough derangement of a man's being when the tyrannical element has gained the mastery, do we trace in the Grecian despot of old! He is depicted as one in whom a single absorbing passion has gradually become predominant. His nobler qualities are crushed and enslaved. His soul is rent by perturbation, anxiety, and remorse. He is full of all kinds of cravings which he is ready to satisfy at any price, but which never are, or are destined to be, satisfied. He is a prey to abject terrors and convulsions, so that if the heart of the tyrant could be opened, it would be found full of wounds and lacerations inflicted by an evil conscience. He cannot abdicate, from fear of those whom he has injured. If one penetrates beneath his outward pomp, he is seen to be the most poverty-stricken of beings.

Such is Plato's description of the despot,[1] through which there runs an analogy between the government of a state that has been broken in upon, and the little commonwealth in man's constitution, where the lower and subordinate faculties have prevailed over the rational and ruling principle. Is it too much,

[1] Rep. ix. 580.

dear brethren, to apply this to Sin? And if elsewhere[1] the same philosopher—when thinking of the effect produced on untrained minds by the popular assemblies at Athens, with their indiscriminate praise and blame—could ask what education was to save the young men of his day from being swept away by the tide of public opinion,—with how much greater solicitude must the Christian minister and anxious tutor of the present day ask, what is to preserve those entrusted to him, when he looks out upon the ferment and tide of eager life in this place, and when he reflects upon the ordeal which they must pass in later years, and upon the everlasting interests that are at stake hereafter? There are stages in the progress of this tyranny of Sin. By God's mercy it is not at once or till after frequent struggles that a man is brought beneath its yoke. There is a time when little transgressions lie heavy on the conscience, and when their load cannot be lightened without instant acknowledgment, reparation, and forgiveness. And well it is for us if we do not resist this call to amendment. There is a later and a sadder stage, when it is far harder to burst the bonds of engrained habit: when it clings round its victim, and cannot be laid aside.

Sin is in truth a hard master; one conces-

[1] Rep. vi. 492.

sion to him invariably demands another. And what mental misery does it entail! The memory of a shameful deed, what torture is that! and if not confessed and repented of, what tenfold torture to him that harbours it!

If then, dear brethren, the thraldom of Sin is so real and unmistakable, so subtle and insidious in its approaches, so deadly in its poison, so potent and permanent in its results, as to make God our Father hide his face for ever from it,—what are the *restorative influences* by which we may hope to be freed from our mortal foe into the liberty of the glorified state of the children of God?

First, do we enough consider what it is to be a Christian? Do we enough prize our position? Do we realize this vital truth, that since Christ came on earth in our form, we are no longer helplessly and irretrievably sold to Sin as bondmen. *He* has done that for our nature which cuts off from it the excuse that it cannot choose but fall. A Christian may be overtaken in a fault, by ignorance, by infirmity, but he must rise at once and go straight to the source of strength. "If any should commit a sin,"[1] says St. John, "we have an Advocate with the Father;" but in the next chapter we read, "he that doeth

[1] ἐάν τις ἁμάρτῃ (the aorist).—1 John, ii. 1.

sin,"—lives a sinful life—not as an occasional lapse, but as a wilful habitual deliberate self-surrender, he " is of the Devil."

No Christian can live in any known evil habit, daily or constantly practised. It is a contradiction in terms to say that such a state is possible. This, then, is one reason why so many fall : they make light of and therefore forfeit the divine image in which they have been recreated. "As many as received him, to them gave he power to become the sons of God." And a *second* reason is that they shun the medicine which they need, and refuse such helps as Prayer. Why are we here, to-day, dear brethren, but that besides offering up praise and thanksgiving, we may address our wants to one who knows them, and who can and will supply them, as is most expedient, if only we ask aright? Can we wonder that in one form or another evil should win an entrance into the citadel if it is left unguarded? I would earnestly ask those whose voices are silent during the Confession—have they ever really thought what confession is?—that it must be the utterance of the individual heart. Do they really fancy that they can confess by deputy? No! "Therein the patient must minister to himself."

And if this last cause of failure is the result of thoughtless indifference, there is another which is more deliberate, and more fatal, springing from a *despair* of the possibility of any signal victory. In some it assumes the form of an indolent palliation of admitted faults. " I am not worse than others." " I shall not be judged individually." In others it settles down, after something of a struggle, into a compromise. " If I cannot conquer this or that failing, as my experience tells me I cannot, I will live up to the highest standard of which I am capable," the result being a tacit concession to some deep-seated habit, perhaps *the very one* with which the contest should *never* be relaxed.

Or again, it takes the more dangerous form of a belief that *none* can be holy, that all in some direction or other drift helplessly before Sin. Scarcely any delusion of the Tempter is more deadly. One decisive answer is given by the biographies of good men. No candid mind can reject the evidence that *many* by God's grace *have* at all times successfully resisted unto the end.

Had Sin dominion over Joseph in his Egyptian, or over Daniel in his Babylonian temptation? Had Sin dominion over Saul of Tarsus when he was at first a blasphemer and a persecutor? or after his conversion, in sharp differences with his dearest friends, in struggles against his thorn in the flesh (whatever that trial was) in his thirty years of missionary toil, did he give place, and not steer right onward for his haven? You remember when provoked to an outburst of resentment, before the Sanhedrin, how immediately and how gracefully he retracted his hasty expression!

Had Sin dominion over the great St. Augustine? No! It could not vanquish him, though in early life he passed through the agonies of a terrible crisis until the memorable day of his baptism at Milan. It could not lead him captive, in spite of the waywardness of his boyhood, in spite of evil associates and evil courses in later youth, of wild opinions adopted afterwards for a time. All this and more we read in those imperishable Confessions, the chief reason for writing which was (he tells us) to praise God for raising him from such a depth, "lest any other might sleep in despair, and say, 'I cannot awake!'"[1] Oh! what a record is *that* of the internal struggle of the soul! what a lesson of intense earnestness! Nor can we forget that God's gratuitous gift of grace (spoken of in the text) was the vital truth, to enforce which Augustine devoted his long life and his mighty intellect.

Or turn from Augustine to one who, ten centuries later, was largely influenced by his

[1] "Confessions," Bk. ii. ch. iii., and Bk. x. ch. iii.

works. Had Sin dominion over Luther? And yet his passions were naturally strong. He was distinguished from other youths of his age only by the greater power of his feelings and the vividness of his imagination. And when, from the sudden death of a friend, and from deep disquietude about himself, he sought the shelter of a cloister, he did not thereby shut out temptation. The natural bent of his character was not towards monasticism; and had he not resisted strenuously, the formalities and mock-religion of the convent might have carried him too away, and silenced the voice which was to change the face of Europe. But he triumphed over sin, first in himself, and so was enabled to re-light the dying lamp of Christendom. What was it which constituted the turning point in his religious history? It was the gaining access to what is open to you and to me, and, alas! how little prized! In the Library at Erfurt he had discovered a book which he had hitherto known only in fragments. It was a Latin Bible, and in *that Bible* it has been said with truth, *was hid the Reformation.*

Once more, to come to our own country, had sin dominion over the stainless virtue of Bishop Ken? That good man exhibited as near an approach to the perfect Christian ideal as has probably ever been reached. Courage and meekness were united in him in a degree seldom paralleled. His lot was cast in most difficult scenes: in a dissolute court, and in an age of faithlessness and want of love. It was no slight task to live innocently and consistently as he did under three successive monarchies: to rebuke, like another John the Baptist, the profligacy of one sovereign, and on his deathbed to call him solemnly to repentance; before another to bear undaunted testimony to the truth, and to suffer imprisonment for it; under a third, to relinquish his bishopric rather than abandon his principles. And what was the clue which guided Ken through the labyrinth of those three reigns? It was the abiding sense of God's presence, which cast out (as the rival force of any virtuous habit steadily cultivated will ever cast out) evil. It was the Love of God which grew with his growth, bore fruit in the love of man, and dictated to him those Morning and Evening Hymns (composed in the first instance for the scholars of Winchester) which will live as long as the English tongue endures. And in our own times may we not point to many who unmistakably refute the shallow fallacy that *all* succumb to the corruption of their nature? Had sin dominion over the lofty zeal and the unwearied energy of Arnold? over the gentle and saintly spirit of Keble?

over the ardent, the fearless, the self-sacrificing Robertson?

But you will say that these are heroic characters far transcending our ordinary experience. I reply that they were men of like passions with ourselves; that out of weakness they were made strong; that their excellence was the fruit of many a conflict, and that they possessed that invariable attendant upon real nobility of character, a constant sense of their own infirmities. St. Paul calls himself, with reference to his former life, the chief of sinners. St. Augustine prays earnestly and repeatedly for deliverance from his own lower nature. "*Libera me a me!*" And Luther's doubts and misgivings were often so serious that at times they amounted to a belief that he was lost.

Sin shall not have dominion over YOU—if you likewise persevere. The very same weapons that they plied are yours; the same words of eternal life; the same Holy Spirit to strengthen and to sanctify you; the same Redeemer with whom you may have communion. If their special crown may not be ours, we still may and must press on for a place (however lowly it may be) in one of those many mansions which He has gone to prepare for them and for us. I most earnestly warn you who are younger—as you would desire the retrospect of an innocent boyhood

—not to trust any who may tell you that the life of hearty work, of sustained diligence, of sober self-control, is irksome or contemptible, instead of being the *only* life that deserves the name of a happy life. I warn you again not to tamper with anything doubtful, anything that will not bear the light of day, or in doing so to shelter yourselves under the miserable plea, too often advanced, "*Others* older, *others* better, have done the same before me." A day is assuredly coming when we shall not be asked *if any* or *how many* have preceded us in a course of evil; but when *the* question of questions will be, whether we have taken pains to enlighten our conscience, and to follow whithersoever its plain directions lead us. I charge you who are older, as you would not hear their voice of agony upbraiding you hereafter, to pause, before you pass on to others, the lurid torch of some corrupt tradition, when you may hold out the steady and starlike beacon of a good example, the averter of many and many a spiritual shipwreck.

I entreat you once more, *never* by hint or innuendo—much less by definite act or incitement—to make one of these little ones to offend, and cause their guardian angels in heaven to relinquish this their sacred charge.

Surely this day, dear brethren, calls on us

all to pass in review before the tribunal of our hearts and memories the months that are irrevocably gone by.

We have reached the end of the Christian year. Another Sunday, and the trumpet-call of Advent will again be summoning us to put on the armour of light. Oh, what a solemn thought that for some here it may be *impossible* to see another, that for some of *us* the next and only Advent will be *Christ's second Advent in glory!* Whatever we believe of "that divine event, to which the whole creation moves," one thing is certain, that Good must triumph everlastingly. But what if sin be then found to have dominion over us? We cannot then change sides, if we are not already marshalled in the ranks of the Conqueror. And there will then be no place found for neutrals. May we so struggle now, dear brethren, against sin, that that *Dies Iræ*, as it must be to the false-hearted, to the coward and the renegade, may be a *Dies Gratiæ* to you and to me, through Christ, who alone giveth us the Victory!

SERMON IV.

GOD'S FINAL REVELATION OF HIMSELF IN CHRIST.[1]

"God, who at sundry times and in divers manners spake in time past unto the fathers by the prophets, hath in these last days spoken unto us by his Son."—*Hebrews*, i. 1.

THE majestic opening of the Epistle to the Hebrews cannot fail to strike the most careless reader. The student of the Greek Testament cannot overlook its faultless structure, its euphonious rhythm, its evenly-balanced periods. The thoughtful reader cannot but find in it abundant material for meditation. It forms a fit prelude to the great Epistle to which, from the uncertainty of its authorship, there attaches something mysterious, going forth (as has been said [2]), like the Melchizedek whom it describes, in lonely, royal, and sacerdotal dignity. We know not with positive assurance whence it cometh, nor whither it goeth. All is in harmony with

---

[1] Quinquagesima Sunday, February 23rd, 1873.
[2] Delitzsch.

its solemn and superhuman subject. It at once arrests our attention, it draws it away from lower objects, and fixes it upon lofty and unearthly truths. These grand opening words look back to the remotest ages of the past; they look forward also to the end of time. They speak of the earlier, less distinct, more partial revelations to men of old, and then of God's later, final crowning revelation of a Son.

While we compare these revelations with each other we must not press their differences too far. For the historical continuity, the substantial identity underlying them, as well as the broad contrast between them, is implied in the text. The various manifestations of God are brought as it were into a focus in the transcendent brilliance of the Gospel light.

In many portions then (for such is the more adequate rendering) and *in divers manners*, *i.e.*, not all at once nor uniformly in the same way, but in many distinct fragments and after manifold fashions did God speak to the fathers of old in the prophets; while he spake at the close of that long period of the world's history to their successors, and to all mankind through all succeeding times, as he speaks to us, too, in our generation, *in His Son*, who is above angel, above prophet, above priest: "whom he appointed heir of all things, by whom also he made the worlds; who, being the brightness of his glory, and the express image of his person, and upholding all things by the word of his power, when he had by himself purged our sins, sat down on the right hand of the Majesty on high."

Think, first, what is included in the very notion of a Revelation—the unveiling of an Infinite Being to the Finite; of the Divine to the Human; of the Eternal to those whose thoughts and actions are, and must be, limited by time; the disclosure of things of perfect beauty, perfect truth, perfect harmony, to beings conscious that they are imperfect; the unfolding of a world hidden from the natural, but discernible to the spiritual eye.

In a lower sense of the word other revelations no doubt there have been. God, who is Love, God, who made man in His own image, we must believe, could not but from the first reveal so much of His nature as it was necessary for His creatures to know. "He left not Himself without witness" (as St. Paul reminded the men of Lystra) "in that he did good and gave us rain from heaven, filling our hearts with food and gladness."

In the beauty and order of the universe (the κόσμος, as the Greeks learnt to call it) who could fail to interpret the symbols of a fatherly interest and a providential care? Men might abuse the lesson, as they did by deifying the powers and properties of nature, or, as in Chaldæa and Persia, by worshipping the stars of heaven, which shine so brilliantly in that clear atmosphere: but still the Divine purpose remained firm. It was that they might seek after the Lord, if haply they might feel after Him and find Him, and recognize in Him the sole sustainer of their existence.

And a further Revelation (however faint it may have become at times and in places) must have reached every tribe and every individual. I mean in natural affection. The instinctive love of parents and children, of brothers and sisters, the bonds of devoted friendship, the mutual concessions required to insure any social harmony, must have led men on to grasp, in some measure, the great truths of a Common Father who is in Heaven.

Such broken lights of the one perfect ray there were. But all such teaching, whether of natural theology or of natural affection, was necessarily imperfect, for it contained in itself no sufficient element of hope, no promise of a higher enlightenment. When, however, we turn to the chosen race, we are struck at once by this broad difference. We trace a design pervading the Scriptures. We see God deigning to reveal Himself more and more in modes intelligible to the human mind, and that, too, in a constantly progressive order.

I would ask you, dear brethren, to follow me in dwelling upon a few of the diverse manners in which God educated His people.

God spake to the patriarchs in ways in which He still speaks to us when our hearts are hardened by prosperity, distracted by doubt, or lifted up by self-reliance. The trials by which Abraham and Isaac were brought nearer to Him in their wanderings and chequered fortunes; the lessons of suffering in his own family by which Jacob was made to see at last the folly of timidity and the misery of deceit; these are not without their counterpart in the severe but merciful accents in which we, too, " in these last days," can often recognize the voice of God. This is a form of the Divine training for which the world never grows too old or too wise. This gives the Scriptures their undying interest; this stamps them with the seal of genuine truthfulness.

Have you, too, my friends, not felt something of this yourselves? How, if one method of the Divine discipline fails to touch your heart, then in another and yet another tone God addresses you? If you have not been pricked by the still small voice of conscience, in moments of quiet reflection; if you have ever slighted the voice of friendly counsel, often repeated, then the Great Teacher Himself comes to you and speaks to you in a different and an unmistakable language, by sickness perhaps, perhaps by disappointment, by the loss of something on which you have set your heart. By one or by many of these or similar channels, God's message does at last reach us to win us to Him, if by any means it may be before it be too late.

This portion of our subject, *the training of life*, as shown in the Old Testament, is boundless. We can but glance at it. The exile of Joseph ; the rise of Moses, out of weakness made strong ; the half-heartedness and insincerity of Balaam ; the habitual converse with God begun in early childhood by Samuel ; the anarchy of conflicting impulses in the wayward spirit of Saul ; the troubles brought upon himself by David ;—these are but a few of the most obvious instances of the way in which God *spake unto the fathers in times past*, in and through the incidents of their lives. The more we study them, the more we see that He did not do so only in the graver and (as we fancy) more critical moments of life, but that quite as often it was on their behaviour under the simplest and most ordinary circumstances that their characters hinged and by them that their destiny was determined

We might pursue the train of thought still further, and note how God spoke not only to individuals, but to the nation. How he proved his people by their long Egyptian servitude, drawing them closer to each other by their sense of a common suffering, drawing them closer to Him, and penetrating them with the belief in His Unity, in contrast with the idolatries they witnessed. How he led them through the desert, in spite of relapses and discontent; granting them one blessing, denying them another. How during the lawless and turbulent period of the Judges He drew out their patriotism, and deepened their trust in a Heavenly Protector. How He concentrated their power and developed their resources under the monarchy, but yet again and again reminded them of a kingdom not of this world by all the misery in which they were so often entangled through their rulers.

They lose their unity so dearly won; again they suffer bondage; again they repent; again they are restored, in part at least, to Palestine. Such is the training spread over many centuries, now by prosperity, now by adversity, by dissatisfaction with their state, and longings after "a better, that is a heavenly country."

Thus did God speak to them by the lessons of life and the education of history.

But beyond this, and in more special ways, were deep truths conveyed to the fathers. Not all at once, but part by part, and as they were able to bear it, was the fulness of God's face revealed. "Thou spakest sometimes in visions unto thy Saints." In visions to the patriarchs, by a more direct, but still by an imperfect and partial mode of revelation, did He speak to Moses.

To different persons and at important epochs did He gradually unfold His nature by the various *Names* by which He proclaimed His Being, to one as the Almighty, the Strong One—to another as *I am*, the Eternal, the Unchangeable One—to another as the Lord of Hosts.

Above all, as ages rolled on, more and more clearly was the value of *goodness* revealed —of honesty of heart and intention—the utter worthlessness, in the sight of God, of outward respectability if unaccompanied by inward purity. In the infancy of the nation these lessons were less dwelt upon. A standard for which they were not ripe was not forced upon them. Step by step were they led up at last to higher conceptions. Still, to Moses, God declared Himself to be " merciful and gracious, long suffering and abundant in goodness and truth," and from Moses to Isaiah and Micah, and from Isaiah to Malachi, there is the same unfaltering assurance that "He dwells in the high and holy place, with him also that is a of a contrite spirit," that what He requires is "to do justly and to love mercy, and to walk humbly with him."

Need I quote those stirring protests in the Psalter against mere formal worship? Are not those warnings of abiding force now "in these last days?"

Such are some of the various ways in which Divine Truth was brought home to the Israelites by the Prophets, that is (to use the title in its widest sense) by the interpreters and expounders of God's will, whose hearts were overflowing, as the word "prophet" implies, with the heavenly message they were inspired to impart.

But we must hasten on to what is of vital importance. We must apply the latter part of the text to our own lives.

Has *God in these last days spoken to us by His Son?* In Him were centred all those yearnings after a Deliverer (which became more and more plain) all that growing belief in an immortal life of the soul—all those visions of a reign of peace and holiness anticipated by the "goodly fellowship of the Prophets." In none of *them* did God speak fully and finally as He did in Christ. Of none of them could it be said, without blasphemy,

"This is my beloved Son in whom I am well pleased." For in Him was absolute goodness —not goodness only in some aspects; not the perfection only of wisdom in words and teaching; but the perfection of love and sympathy in active life, the one ideal sacrifice exhibited in a human person.

Our own times are included in *these last days*. The revelation of God in Christ, though final, is capable of infinite expansion. It meets the wants of all ages, all circumstances, all characters. It proposes one aim, one ideal to rise, through Divine power, superior to temptation, to live after the pattern of Christ.

It is not like those fossil palms and ferns which long ago grew in luxuriant beauty, but are now rigid and sapless in their stony prison. No, it contains within itself a growing principle of life. The Gospel of the Hebrew Christians of the first century is the Gospel equally of the nineteenth century. The Gospel of the darkest ages of ignorance—of the time, for instance, of the accession of Alfred, when not a single priest south of the Thames understood the ordinary prayers, or could translate Latin into his mother tongue, is still the same Gospel which speaks to us, armed with all the resources of modern learning, and with all the latest aids of textual criticism accumulated since the last revision.

Yes, all our fresh springs must be in it! Do not misunderstand me. The study of it cannot indeed work a miracle in us; it is not by itself a universal remedy—much else must go with it. But I say that the more we read Old or New Testament, reverentially, thoughtfully, prayerfully, the more clearly shall we discern a divine hand guiding us, and hear a divine voice suggesting to us "new thoughts of God, new hopes of heaven."

Let me, then, ask you in all seriousness, *has God spoken to you yet by His Son?* By all that He did to ennoble our nature and to show us what it might become? Has he spoken to tutors and pupils to labour together for one common, one lofty end? Has He spoken to you to put away follies, to consecrate to Him this coming Lent? Is there *nothing* you can do for Him during it? Surely there is very much for all—for the youngest of us—to do. Oh those harsh and hasty judgments we pass on persons and motives—so hateful in the sight of our merciful Father, the righteous Judge, who is strong and patient though He is provoked every day; so contrary to the charity which (as we have just read) "is not easily provoked, thinketh no evil, rejoiceth not in iniquity but rejoiceth in the truth."

Oh that specious show of work, the fruit of

another's brain! Oh those flimsy evasions and prevarications which gained you, perhaps, a slight and superficial advantage, but which wounded the moral sense deeply, perhaps mortally!

Oh that purpose to work which never is but always *to be* accomplished! Oh that indolent saunter to questionable, unprofitable, if not actually forbidden haunts! Oh that relapse into the mire of sin, when we thought that our feet were now at last upon the Rock! Oh that debt, which it is vain to try to fill up while you constantly pour in more, a self-renewing trouble, worse than the leaky vessel of the fabled daughters—a woe for future years! How long, how long shall these things be? Is there no escape? Yes! Will you not come to the Great Physician? His touch has still its ancient power; He and He alone can restore to you the years that the cankerworm has eaten.

The time may come, remember, when the Book may be spread before us, but it will be like song to the deaf, or like characters in an unknown tongue. What then will all else avail? For lastly, my friends, if God has not yet spoken to us convincingly in His Son, while Scepticism is speaking to the intellect, questioning Gospel truth, and banishing every vestige of the supernatural as if it were a superfluous intrusion, or while Fashion is speaking to our affections and enticing them away, what avails it that we are the heirs of all the ages? Can all our boasted civilization minister to a troubled conscience? Thankful, deeply thankful should we be that we live now. But let us never forget that

> "all those trophied arts
> Heal'd not a passion or a pang
> Entail'd on human hearts."

Be the thoughts of man ever so much widened, be our culture ever so refined, if we rest on these things alone "it profiteth us nothing." Whether the past have its prophecies, they belong to time, and with it they shall cease; whether there be knowledge, the accumulated treasures of "these last days," the treasures yet to be gathered in, in days far hence, when we are gone—knowledge, too, precious as it is, shall vanish away. It shall serve its turn; its place shall be taken by other knowledge. It shall finally be lost and merged in the higher knowledge of God, who is Love. Love alone is imperishable. In it what we now see through a glass darkly we shall then see face to face. All that now perplexes the mind, all that now baffles and disappoints the heart in our conflict with evil, shall be solved. If we must be content "to know in part," where even the wisest cannot pierce the veil, at least the light shines clear and steady on the path of daily duty. "The secret of the Lord is with them that fear Him." May our prayer be daily, "Speak, Lord, for Thy servant heareth." And oh may no wiles of the evil one, no sophistry of man, no deceitfulness of self ever drown that Voice, or draw us away from following it, whithersoever it would lead us!

Sermon V.
PERMANENCE AMIDST CHANGE.[1]

"They shall perish, but thou shalt endure: yea, all of them shall wax old like a garment; as a vesture shalt thou change them, and they shall be changed; but thou art the same, and thy years shall have no end."—*Psalm* cii. 26, 27.

MANY deep thoughts are suggested to us by this and the two following Psalms. They breathe the language of spiritual security, the sense of trustful gladness in seasons of happiness, of resignation in seasons of depression. The greatness, and at the same time the tenderness of God, the beauty, the multiplicity, the complexity of the wonderful objects of this earth, the absolute dependence of all living creatures on their Maker, find here perhaps their noblest expression.

But two thoughts stand out prominently through them. First, there is the thought of the One Unchangeable Being, in sharp contrast with the vanishing objects of sense. And next, in the verse immediately following the text, there is another great thought: namely, that in spite of the mutability of all created things, still

[1] May 18th, 1873.

there is something even here which has in it an element of permanence, and a ground of hope: "The children of thy servants shall continue, and their seed shall be established before thee."

To reflect on the unchangeable Deity is one of those vast and overpowering reflections which seem at times almost to appal us when we try to dwell steadily upon it. It is like the idea of the infinity of space, which our minds can neither grasp nor yet refuse to accept. When we look out on the starry heavens, sown with countless worlds beyond worlds, we cannot conceive that space can be bounded: for the mind at once overleaps any limit that we imagine, however immeasurable the distance at which we fix it. Nor, again, can we picture to ourselves the illimitable. It is like it in its overpowering intensity. But it is a far profounder thought, and one on which it is far more profitable to dwell, and to realize it so far as we may do so; for this reason, that it sets us upon meditating on a Being, and not on any one of His creations. It brings before us One who is unchangeable in His perfection, unchangeable in His attributes, unchangeable therefore in His attitude towards good and towards evil.

It is from this point of view that I would ask you to consider the subject of the text. I would attempt to bring home to you the practical bearing of the text and deepen the sense of what is beyond doubt, and to mark out some reasons why it is good for us, again and again, to pause in our hurried course to meditate upon the One unwearied worker, and remember the great truth that God is Immutable, and that with Him is no variableness, neither shadow caused by change.

That we and all around us are frail and mutable, never continuing in one stay, we know full well; but do we not put the thought away from us, and do we not fail to profit by it as we might do? We see the great Law written upon all we behold. The solid earth, what changes has it witnessed! The waves of ocean roll over spots where the busy tide of human life once ebbed and flowed. The hillsides, now clothed with vegetation, were once tenanted by the creatures of the great deep. Again, what is all history, we may say, but the chronicle of constant change? Of progress, as we trust, towards a higher and a better state of things; but, however we may regret it, of change, of the abandonment of what is antiquated and outworn, of the removal of what was long believed to be fixed and durable, of the gradual melting away of the past into the present? Look at the change in our bodies. Their daily waste is constantly being repaired; so much so that they are different from what they were in childhood, or a few years ago. Our habits of thought, our tempers and hearts are not exactly such as they once were.

In this scene, within us and without us, of incessant change, oh! what a salutary, what a sustaining, what a comforting and ennobling thought is the grand one of the text, "Thou art the same."

It is, first, a very *humbling* reflection, sobering and solemnizing our lives. What are all our little systems, our ambitious schemes, our eager wishes and fears,

> "those unsolid hopes
> Of happiness, those longings after fame,
> Those restless cares, those busy bustling days,"

which were so intensely important at the time? What are they in the retrospect? Weighed in the balance of calmer judgment, how paltry and insignificant do they appear! The only part worthy to last is what has in any way promoted God's will. And how marred by imperfection, by vanity, or self-love, is the utmost that the best of us can perform! When we review the past do we not feel that God was not in the earthquake or the fire of our trepidation and anxiety, but that He was and is in the still small voice of conscience which it is ours to slight or to obey? He has been constant while we have been eddying to and fro. He rules the troubled sea of our disquietude. He sitteth above the waterflood of our frequent relapses, our wilfulness and presumption. He will guide our restless bark into the haven where we would be, if we will only commit it to Him, and not shape our self-chosen course according to our own fancies. Consider, too, for a moment, how shallow, how hasty our judgments often are: how the experience of a few years reverses a sentence pronounced with the utmost confidence. The estimate of all but a very few of the most celebrated characters and reputations is perpetually being re-examined, sifted, and corrected by later criticism. The next time, therefore, we are tempted to defer blindly to current opinion or popular applause, let us pause and ask ourselves, Is this to which I am paying the homage of my heart worthy of it—is this the judgment that would be passed by the most enlightened—is it, above all, in harmony with the Divine Will? "But the counsel of the Lord shall endure for ever." The broad distinctions of right and wrong are absolutely unalterable. The angry thought, the passionate word or deed of yesterday, is as hateful in His sight as was the sin of Cain.

And secondly, what a *comforting* thought is this, "Thou are the same." It consoled Moses after his forty years of seemingly fruitless toil, when he sang, "Lord, thou hast been our refuge from one generation to another"—that inspired hymn which is still fresh and strong after thousands of years, with the freshness and strength of imperishable truth, and which day after day to the mourners still breathes the same unfaltering trust and the same primal sympathy.

This thought reassured the author of the 77th Psalm, when, in his momentary despondency, he said, "Hath God forgotten to be gracious?" It consoled St. Paul when, though his prayer was not literally granted, he heard Christ say, "My grace is sufficient for thee, for my strength is made perfect in weakness." It has cheered every earnest seeker after God in high or low estate. It has nerved saints and martyrs, statesmen and poets—the sick bowed down by affliction, the vigorous baffled and perplexed by their failure to extirpate evil. When all visible help is gone, then does resignation cling closer to the invisible.

When wave after wave of trial has passed over a man, is it consolation to tell him that others have suffered, or are now suffering similarly? Is it comforting to talk to him of the uniformity of the laws of nature, or to remind him that a particular course of action must lead to a corresponding result? It is indeed most true. The laws of matter and of mind are inexorable. They cannot be trifled with. Their regularity forms the most striking exception to the fleeting scenes around us. But on whom depend those invariable sequences of phenomena, in which we know no break and no pause? The words immediately preceding the text give us the answer: "Thou, Lord, in the beginning hath laid the foundation of the earth, and the heavens are the work of thy hands." Those laws are unerring; sustained by their author, the lawgiver, during His pleasure. But not on laws alone, though of the utmost wisdom, can we rest. No, it is on a person we must lean: "Our heart and our flesh cry out for the living God." There is genuine, truest comfort in the recollection, "Thou art the same." All this past, with its mistakes and its follies, has taught me to see this more clearly, to be dissatisfied with self. Leave me not, now I have found Thee, to my own fickle and treacherous heart. Guide me, uphold me, stablish me!

Again, thirdly, "Thou art the same" is a *stimulating*, an elevating thought.

It bids us never be satisfied, never be self-complacent. We have a Father in heaven who is perfect; we have an ideal Life in the Gospel, after which we are to struggle, "faint yet pursuing." Forwards! Forwards! and Upwards!

is the Christian's watchword. It is only the lowest and poorest minds that rest content with what they have already accomplished. Higher and nobler natures feel that the ideal they have had before them nothing can truly represent. The hour of their greatest success will be the hour when they feel this most keenly. To rest content with what it has achieved is fatal to true genius.

There is a story told of the Danish sculptor Thorwaldsen,[1] which may be read in the spirit of St. Paul's words, "not as though I had already attained, or were made perfect," how a friend found him one day in low spirits. Being asked whether anything had distressed him, he answered : " My genius is decaying." "What do you mean?" said the visitor. "Why! here is my statue of Christ," he replied ; "it is the first of my works that I have ever felt satisfied with. Till now my idea has always been far beyond what I could execute. But it is no longer so. *I shall never have a great idea again.*" It is indeed the glorious prerogative of God, to be able to look down upon His Creation, and behold that it was very good.

But we still must ask how and to whom is the thought of God's unchangeableness a

---

[1] See "Guesses at Truth," 1871, p. 59.

solemnizing, a comforting, an ennobling one? If you are the slave of one known evil habit, it cannot be so: for then the thought of His unchangeable attitude towards sin will be as a consuming fire. It will terrify you by the everlasting rebuke it gives to the contradiction your lives are presenting to Him. Or again, if He is as yet nothing but a vague and remote abstraction to you, if you have never regarded yourselves as standing in any definite and close relation to Him, to think of Him can no more bring healing to you, than to meditate over any abstract scientific truth can do so. It is only when you are penetrated with the belief that He loves you with a love such as words cannot describe, that you can repose upon the Everlasting Arms; it is not till we can exclaim with Isaiah from our hearts, "Doubtless Thou art our Father,—Thou, O Lord, art our Father, our Redeemer," that we can bear the contrast between the sin-blurred image of our lives, and His glorious and unfading perfection.

But there remains another aspect of our subject too important to be omitted. Is there nothing in our nature but what is shifting and changing perpetually? Is there nothing in it permanent and undecaying?

All that has ever been said or done by the

good and the wise of old (so far as it partakes of the everlasting attributes of the Deity), "those truths that wake to perish never," we may believe will last and triumph. And, more than this, whatever we have done, whether for good or evil, remains in its effects. It has shaped us and made us what we are at the present moment.

The earnest prayer for others, the hour which you devoted to some good act when you were tempted, perhaps, to squander it upon trivial or sensual pleasure, the word of warning which it was so hard to speak out, but which you did speak out in season to your friend—all these remain. Like the ripples traced by geology upon what are now far inland sands—so do those past actions remain indelibly imprinted on the character. Their living result in confirmed habit points as plainly to past struggles, as those ancient wave-marks point to the existence of seas which have long since vanished.

But apart from the intrinsic colour and character of our actions, is there not something else which is permanent and inseparable from our being?—Yes! there is the awful but indisputable fact of *Personal Identity*.

"There is (to borrow Bishop Butler's language[1]) the conviction which necessarily and

---

[1] Dissertation X., On Personal Identity.

every moment rises within us, when we turn our thoughts upon ourselves, and reflect upon that which is ourself now, and that which was ourself twenty years ago, that they are not two but one and the same self: the consciousness that we are the same agents or living beings now which we were as far back as our remembrance reaches."

Oh what a marvellous thing is this Personal Identity! To think that it can survive, can bridge over the broad gulfs which seem to separate portions of a life! Think to what an abyss man can sink! *"Grande profundum est ipse homo."*[1] Could David, the ingenuous shepherd-boy, fall as low as he afterwards did? Could Peter, indeed, deny his Master and his Friend? Could Constantine yield so fatally to jealousy and passion as, on a groundless charge and untried to execute his son Crispus? Could the noble-minded Theodosius give his sanction to the frightful massacre at Thessalonica? Could the great Bacon have been guilty of corruption and venality?

Alas, such are the possibilities of our nature when left to itself. We can often recognize here the sharply defined differences in char-

[1] Augustine, Conf., Lib. IV. xiv.

acter which an interval will produce. That boy who came among us so fresh and unsullied, recollecting and repeating the prayer learnt at his mother's knee; can he be the same that we see after a few brief school-times so grievously altered? That stubborn disposition, on the other hand, once so difficult to rouse, or influence, so vapid, so unprofitable, so impracticable, can it have been transfigured, as by God's grace it has been, into the thoughtful, orderly, diligent, and considerate character? That youth who seemed so hopeless and intractable, can he (as we say) be the same person? Yes, he is the very same in all that constitutes his essential being. He is not the same in the direction which his chastened will has taken, in his language, his demeanour, in the whole tone and tenor of his daily life. But in his power to choose the evil or the good, in his relation to his Maker, in a word in his Responsibility, he is and ever will remain the same.

O shall we not then do well to pray for *perseverance* in goodness? Shall we not strive that our days may be "bound each to each by natural piety?" For holiness, while life lasts, is exposed to the merciless and unremitting attacks of the evil one, with all his versatile resources. Specially during the earlier stages of its growth is it a delicate and sensitive flower, needing the most tender nurture and the most careful vigilance. Transplanted from the pure atmosphere of home to scenes of ruder and sterner experience it must encounter much to imperil it. Coldness and contempt may freeze and nip it in the bud. Fashion or tradition may easily trample it down and succeed in crushing the life out of it. The contagious breath of pernicious example may scatter over it a poisonous blight.

But Christ's prayer for his own was, " I pray not that thou shouldest take them out of the world, but that thou shouldest keep them from the evil." There is no necessary reason why holiness should not survive such dangers, why the soil of Eton should be less congenial to it than the soil of home, or why her sons should not "grow up as the young plants;" why a Christian boyhood should not here burgeon and blossom into a robuster type, if only it be watered and trained by daily prayer and penitence, fed by the sacramental graces of Christ, warmed and illuminated by His health-giving rays, and enabled through Him to absorb all the good influences of this place and cast out all the bad. Therefore pray for *perseverance*, the secret of a thousand successes; the antidote to a thousand disappointments, the equivalent, in the wise and merciful economy of Heaven's bounty, for genius and great gifts which many of us cannot have, and which without some measure of it often prove a snare to their possessor.

And lastly, recollect, I beseech you—I say it not to cloud one innocent joy, or check one lofty or legitimate aim, but to temper all with a holier and loftier light—recollect the certainty of the Four Last Things.

Does not the utmost amount of revolution that our fortunes can possibly undergo shrink into absolutely nothing compared with the unutterable transformation in store for us hereafter? for we shall all be changed, we know not how. But we know that through and beyond that crowning change the man himself shall be preserved, shall stand before his Maker, in his incommunicable identity.

May it be ours to enter then on that sphere of happy labour and of holy love: labour that shall fear no languor, no discouragement, no failure; love that shall feel no yearning unsatisfied, together with those whom we have known here in their hour of trial, the spirits of just men now made perfect, whom we cannot think of as subject any longer to decay. May you, may we all be so steadfast and unmovable, so abounding in the work of the Lord, that when the final, the indelible stamp is set upon the character, we may be sealed as the servants of Him who, change as everything else around us may and does change, is "the same yesterday, to-day, and for ever."

> "But Thou art true, Incarnate Lord,
> Who didst vouchsafe for man to die;
> Thy smile is sure, Thy plighted word
> No change can falsify."

Sermon VI.

THESE THREE YEARS.

"Behold, these three years I come seeking fruit on this fig tree."—*St. Luke*, xiii. 7.

VERY deaf to the appeal made by Scripture to the enlightened conscience must he be who, in these words, can hear nothing addressed to himself. Very hard and literal must that interpretation be which can trace in them a reference to the three successive dispensations under Moses, under the Prophets, and under Christ, but can go no further. There is a depth, an intensity in all Christ's words, which refuses to be imprisoned within such narrow limits. The study of our Saviour's words, searching and minute as it must ever be if we would penetrate below the surface, if it does not descend into the heart, if it fail to touch the springs of action, "profiteth nothing." It will degenerate into a mere verbal study instead of soaring upwards to the life-giving Spirit. There is, however, one among the various interpretatious of the text which claims our more particular consideration. It does seem natural and obvious to find in the three years an allusion to the term of Christ's ministry, the third year of which was now lapsing. For in an especial manner "the owner of the vineyard" by whom, probably, Christ Himself is intended, did then come unto his own, and watch to see what fruits they would bear; and the "dresser of the vineyard," that is the Holy Spirit, at the eleventh hour of their long day of grace, was then specially pleading for them.

But even this view must not be pressed unduly, for there is force in the objection that if a chronological order be sought in the first part of the parable, it ought in equal strictness to be applied to its close. For if the three years denote only our Lord's earthly visitation, then (it is urged with some force) the sentence, "cut it down, why cumbereth it the ground?" would naturally follow, not as it did after an interval of forty years, but in the year that immediately followed its utterance.

Waiving, then, any interpretations which would limit the scope of the parable too narrowly, may we not attach a broader sense to the words? and may we not trace in them that warning Voice which speaks to nations in all the more striking epochs of their existence? and which speaks to us, my friends, in the retrospect of any marked period of our lives, those halting-places so mercifully granted us, those division and landmarks into which the little history of each of us so easily falls—those critical turning-points in the state of each individual soul, which seem to cry aloud to the Christian as he surveys the past,—*Respice, Aspice, Prospice.*

Nations have their special warnings, and to them Christ comes seeking fruit. The Church, too, has had her more momentous periods and stages, when her Master's Voice might seem to have sounded forth more solemnly than at other seasons, in language like that of the Angel in the Apocalypse, "I will come to thee quickly and will remove thy candlestick out of his place, except thou repent." Often and often must the thoughtful student of her annals pause, in wonder and thankfulness at the mercy which has spared her so long and brought her alive out of such trials as she has witnessed. Whether he reflect on her condition at the close of the tenth century, when "men's hearts failed them for fear, and for looking after those things which they deemed were coming upon the earth;" when so widespread was the anarchy and so crushing the misery, that the end of the world was universally expected to be at hand. Whether he recall the degradation of the Papacy both before and after that epoch;

or whether again he come nearer to our own times, and think of the dreary spectacle presented by the eighteenth century, its torpor, its want of faith, when the love of many waxed cold, and, with some rare exceptions, like Wesley, all true religion might seem to have slumbered and slept.

But while the historical element is more or less traceable in most of our Lord's parables, and forms indeed in some of them their prominent feature, their moral value can never be ignored. And the parable before us is, in this respect, one of the most pointed and direct. Its personal application is of paramount importance if we would benefit by it at all. For it is not (observe) the world at large that we have to consider, it is not even any selected portion of it, it is the *one particular tree* planted in it, on which our thoughts are centred. "A certain man had *a fig tree planted in his vineyard;* and he came and sought fruit thereon, and found none. Then said he unto the dresser of his vineyard, Behold, these three years I come seeking fruit on this fig tree, and find none: cut it down; why cumbereth it the ground?—And he answering said unto him, 'Lord, let it alone this year also, till I shall dig about it and dung it, and if it bear fruit, well: and if not, then after that thou shalt cut it down.'"

The opening image, a fig tree in a vineyard strange as it may seem to us, was natural in Palestine, where any trees are allowed to grow freely wherever they can get root ; and it rivets the thought upon the one tree which cannot in the crowd of other trees escape the eye of the owner when he comes to examine his property. He singles out at a glance the unfruitful specimen, the unprofitable individual, who has his station among Christ's trees, with the broad leaves of profession to catch the eye, while devoid of real fruit, and that, too, when basking in the sunshine of his many privileges.

Let us regard our text in this light, bearing in mind the two great thoughts that underlie the parable, God's long-suffering, and God's severity, His mercy and His judgment : the certainty of mercy if we look aright for it, in every moment of our lives; the certainty of judgment, if by apathy and neglect, no less than by active misdeeds, we forfeit the right of appeal to mercy.

These three years. There is an advantage in taking any clear precise period over which the memory can range with less chance of self-deception in its estimate of results. To some they may represent the exact number of years they have spent in this place, or during which they have worshipped in this chapel. To others they have been the last three years of their time here, the close of one distinct period of probation, before the new page of University life is opened with its three years, its increased liberty, its graver temptations, its enlarged opportunities for good.

Ask yourselves candidly, what have I done with these three last years? Can I survey them without misgiving? Am I really at all advanced on my way? If I can look back on some few victories gained, has it been only, after all, in a sudden, fitful, transient emotion for good, or in what alone will stand,—a matured habit of self-control and self-mastery for the highest motive, namely, to conform more and more to my heavenly Master's pattern, and not merely because the contrary has been found by experience in the end to be most troublesome? Is it still a painful effort to do right? or has it at last come to resemble an instinct?

After taking account of many disheartening failures, perhaps of many sad declensions from the high standard I remember to have once set before me, is there a clear gain on the side of improvement? Are the feelings brought more under the guidance of the judgment? Are sloth and temper and passion still the same dangerous enemies that they were three years ago? Not yet vanquished, but constantly mutinous, and clamorously reasserting their dominion? Or have you set any definite plan before you after which you have been building up your character? Are the three years in the retrospect but a chaos of confusion, an unlovely picture, from which you would fain turn away altogether—a tangled web of unchastened wishes, of unreasonable hopes, of eager pursuit after one futile object exchanged for others equally futile? Oh, if so, pause, I pray you! Think—

> "Will God, indeed, with fragments bear,
> Snatched late from the decaying year?"

Will He indeed make allowance in the great account for what is already wasted? *These three years*—Have not the seasons read their lessons to you?

> "three winters cold
> Have from the forests shook three summers' pride;
> Three beauteous springs to yellow autumn turn'd;
> Three April perfumes in three hot Junes burn'd."

As they, in their solemn process, have gradually faded into each other, so are our lives imperceptibly but surely passing through their several stages, and leading us on from one sphere of duty to another.

If they have been years in which your cup of enjoyment has been full and running over, have they brought more thoughtfulness for others perhaps less prosperous than yourselves? More desire to enter into their views, and help them onward by kind deed, by sympathy or suggestion? Have you ever thought of uninterrupted prosperity as involving some danger? Have you ever taken to heart that " unto whomsoever much is given, of the same shall be much required?" Or if, on the other hand, you have had to bear some check or rebuff—have they brought with them a deeper conviction that life is not all enjoyment, that here we can have no continuing city? That fancied slight, that imaginary grievance, has it been seen in its right proportions, and the due amount of blame apportioned to self? Or again, this real and unmistakable trial, which must be looked in the face and met manfully, has it been accepted as part of the Divine scheme by which God is leading us to Him as the Supreme Good?

Thus if we review the years, neither complacently, nor again too despondently, but humbly and sincerely anxious to read them aright, the dry bones of the past will become instinct with life, while the Divine breath passes over them, and will shape themselves with a definite outline into the special lesson they contain for each. Again—*these three years*—how much might we have gained from them in other ways. Mentally, how many difficulties have been surmounted? Ask yourselves. The inveterate persistence in some grammatical error—the inability to grasp and apply some property of numbers, again and again elucidated, how do these things clog and hamper the learner? And is not this as often from a want of thoroughness, of zeal, and of concentrated effort, from a perfunctory way of going through a certain amount of routine, as from any real and rooted impossibility to master the difficulty once and for ever? And to mount to a higher region, granted that the mind has been strengthened and informed—have reverence and humility grown side by side with knowledge? What spiritual harvest has been gathered in from these services worthy to be garnered in the everlasting storehouse? During *these three years* you have heard upwards of one hundred sermons from this pulpit—from strangers and from friends. What permanent influence have their counsels left behind them? Far be it from me to say they have left none, but I would venture to make a suggestion, though to some it may appear too obvious and homely a one to make. If each Sunday some short note or record were kept, were it but the text and a few leading thoughts, the word would be less likely to be spoken in vain. It would, I am convinced, lay a firmer hold upon your memory, and through your memory upon your hearts, and good impressions would less rapidly melt away and evaporate.

But to turn to the last part of the text—'These three years I come seeking fruit." My Christian friends, is it not one of the most solemn questions, What fruit would Christ find in us? Some there must be. If not that of the good then that of the corrupt tree. If not figs or grapes, there will be thorns and thistles, the rank growth of past neglect, the consequences of which are telling on the character at this moment.

Need I dwell on the many passages where the Bible enforces the absolute necessity of fruit? Need I remind you how St. Paul groups the fruits of the spirit under three heads, "love. joy, peace," as an inner settled habit of mind? then "honesty, gentleness, temperance," to guide the whole conduct outwardly; and in our intercourse with others, "long-suffering, kindness, and beneficence." Need I repeat his question to any who have ever been the slaves of lust? "What fruit had ye then?" Did that life repay you, did it leave anything else but shame and remorse and an enfeebled will behind it?

O think, if the Lord were suddenly to come to you, could you abide the day of His coming? Think if He were to come to you whose bodies are consecrated to be His Temple, and surprise you defiling that Temple? or still worse, teaching, encouraging, soliciting another to do so? Or think if He were to find it only swept and garnished, one bad habit having died out, not having been truly cast out by Him; and the chamber standing open and vacant, too ready for another more fatal occupant to enter in and take possession?

Do your studies bear fruit? The answer depends in a large measure on yourselves; in the spirit in which you approach them; on the humility, patience, and self-surrender with which you cultivate portions of the field of knowledge, which may at the first survey appear unattractive, but without which you cannot advance.

Do your friendships bear fruit? On what motives are they founded? Do they lead you into actions or haunts which a few years hence you would willingly forget? Do they stimulate a healthy and rational interchange of thought and debate on those questions which, however old, are of ever fresh and undying interest? Or does conversation too often revolve in a dreary round of petty gossip or personal scandal?

Depend upon it, if our tree does not *fructify,* however showy be the profusion of its foliage, its very existence will be endangered. What we seem to have will be taken away from us. The age in which we live is emphatically a scrutinizing and a *fruit-seeking age*. It is intolerant of shams, of mere leaves. It demands realities. This tendency may at times show too exclusive a devotion to what can be gauged by tangible and immediate results. But in the main it is a good sign, and honest work and empty profession are more than ever rated at their proper value. "Any institution" (it has been truly said) "which will not march is doomed. Any establishment, any order, any work, any individual man, not giving proof of vitality, by growth, by work, by fruit, must sooner or later, and probably soon rather than late, hear the stern mandate, with the axe lying at its root, 'Cut it down : why cumbereth it the ground.'"

Do not let us fancy that we can escape the demand for fruit, or that others will not enter in and reap our inherited advantages, if we are occupying the good soil in vain; if you are not only bearing no fruit on it yourselves, but positively hindering it from rendering the return it might otherwise have rendered. For this is to cumber the ground, to impoverish and exhaust it, to mar and mischief it ; to intercept the blessed air and sunshine, and to draw off and uselessly absorb the fatness and the nourishment around.

And again, let us ask who is the cumberer of the ground, if it be not one who is without a spark of zeal for good: the indifferent spectator rather than the earnest actor in life's solemn drama, the insidious tempter, who with a light jest will impede honest work in another, and break down the barrier of good impressions which has hitherto preserved his innocence?

But there is another aspect of the parable which may not be overlooked, and is implied in the tender intercession of the vine-dresser pleading for the reprieve of another year.

I mean this. Does Christ come only *seeking* fruit? Does He not also *give* the germs, the means of bearing fruit? Does he not freely bestow the sweet influence of His Holy Spirit on those who ask? Is He a hard taskmaster? Does He expect you to grow in goodness, unaided and unrenewed? No! He knows our nature, which He bore Himself, too well for that. "In that he himself hath suffered being tempted, he is able to succour them that are tempted."

But He does expect the offering of our hearts. He "who in the days of his flesh offered up prayers and supplications with strong crying and tears," does expect that when we look into ourselves and find help from within hopeless, we will turn to Him for help, in order to bring forth the fruits of righteousness which are by Jesus Christ. And whether it be in the fresh morning of youth, in the noonday toil and heat of mature life, or after the calm sunset of old age, of each one of us we know that ere very long God will impartially and searchingly and finally demand fruit. As He will come at the end of the ages, at the great ingathering, when the cry shall go forth, "Thrust in thy sickle and reap, for the time is come for thee to reap, for the earth is ripe." Evil will then be no longer permitted to encumber the good ground. The second part of the parable will then be acted out. The term of longsuffering will be past. The hour for judgment will have arrived. Let us all strive with one heart and with one aim to be fellow labourers with Christ (what a noble title!), to be of use in our generation, in the true sense of that oft abused term Utility:

> "At least, not rotting like a weed,
> But, having sown some generous seed,
> Fruitful of further thought and deed,
> To pass, when Life her light withdraws."

Yes! then and then only—for you and for me—if our tree have something to show better than mere leaves, "if it bear fruit *well;*" well in moments of joy and exultation, or it may be in periods of gloom, of disappointment, and depression. Well in glowing health, or, if your Father so wills it, in the sick chamber: well in riches or in poverty, in high or low estate as He shall think best;—well in Time, and well to all Eternity.

SERMON VII.

THE BOOK OF JOB.[1]

"Thou writest bitter things against me, and makest me to possess the iniquities of my youth."—*Job*, xiii. 26.

UPON one of those earliest monuments, the Egyptian sepulchres, there is a representation of a Future Judgment. The deceased person advances to receive his sentence at the throne of the god Osiris. His actions are being weighed in the scales of Truth. Beside them stands a god, his accuser or his advocate, with a tablet in his left hand, and in his right the recording pen. The tribunal of the unseen world is shadowed forth under forms which we know were employed in Egypt from the earliest times, where the writing of the adversary was always produced in court, and read aloud.

Those blurred and faded, yet still surviving, colours speak to us out of the long past ages. And whether we regard them as vestiges of

[1] February 28th, 1875; and at Durham Cathedral, February 18th, 1894.

some very early revelation, or whether we trace them to a belief deeply seated in every human heart, a forecast of a future certainty, in either case, how forcibly do they illustrate those words, "Thou writest bitter things against me."

"Thou writest bitter things against me, and makest me to possess the iniquities of my youth." Yes! Such (varying no doubt in widely differing degrees), must be the universal confession. One, and one only, could ever say "The Prince of this world cometh and hath nothing in me," no weak yielding; no point whereon to fasten his attack. Such must be the universal language of Conscience.

And now reflect what manner of man it was that spoke these words. If of one of the best of men, steadily surveying his former life, they were more or less true, how much more must they be true of many, whose past, as it is out of sight, so it is out of mind; how much more should a passage like this, holding up the mirror of Scripture to the heart and the memory, stir the lethargic and arrest the indifferent, when one who takes his stand upon his general integrity, and will not relinquish it, when even he thus frankly acknowledges his inherent corruption. For Job is described on no less than Divine testimony as "a perfect and upright man, without his like on all the earth," as "one that feared God and eschewed evil." He is brought before us at the opening of that wonderful Book as the friend of the poor, of unaffected piety, humble when in wealth and power, combining in his own person the utmost goodness with the highest degree of earthly happiness. His patience under suffering has passed into a proverb.

The outlines of the story which follows are depicted in colours too vivid to be effaced from the recollection of any who has once read it. Look at the malice of the fiend who in the heavenly council suggests that all this goodness is not disinterested. He is permitted to put forth his hand and try him. Then a storm of successive calamities falls upon him with startling, with bewildering rapidity,—ruin of house, destruction of family, utter desolation. He stands the trial, but a second time the heavenly council is held, and a severer test is allowed to be applied, a fresh stroke felt in his own person. He feels the direst disease of the East in its most malignant form. And last, and far worst of all to a warm and generous heart, the agony caused by the defection of those nearest and dearest to him, the imputation by friends (at first through dark hints, and at last by definite statement), of a plague-spot hidden in his bosom, of a dark undercurrent of crime, concealed beneath the smooth surface of his outward prosperity.[1]

What think you must all this have been! And observe, the sting of the taunt lay in this, that it was grounded on an appearance of truth. Ordinary experience does seem to bear out his friends' accusations. And in those early days there was the traditional belief in a speedy retribution overtaking the wicked. It pervades much of the Psalms. Misery is in most cases the fruit of a vicious life. Prosperity does generally attend Virtue. *Generally*, but not invariably. There lay their mistake in overstating this view of life (in making prosperity an absolute test of God's favour, an indispensable proof of inner righteousness). And in urging this, they are led further and further away from the truth, into intemperate language, while he grows calmer, more collected, and more resigned. We know that virtue is not always rewarded in life; that sorrow and misfortune are often parts of God's dealing with us in ways which *we* can only half understand. We know that they do not necessarily prove the commission of sin, for it is but an imperfect account of them which makes their only object a penal one. They have other and not less precious pur-

[1] Eliphaz specifies inhumanity, avarice, and abuse of power.

poses: to try our faith, to enlighten, and to humble.

But are Job's friends the only persons who have hastily argued from suffering to guilt? Christ himself, you remember, on more than one occasion rebuked such superficial reasoning: "Suppose ye that these Galileans were sinners above all the Galileans, because they suffered such things?" "Or those eighteen on whom the tower in Siloam fell, and slew them, think ye that they were sinners above all men that dwelt in Jerusalem? I tell you, Nay; but except ye repent, ye shall all likewise perish." And again, when asked, "Master, who did sin, this man or his parents, that he was born blind?" did He not check the spirit in which the question was put? "Neither hath this man sinned, nor his parents: but that the works of God should be made manifest in him." Can we be surprised if the complete solution was hidden from Job? It is only in part revealed to us. The answer at last granted was, that God's wisdom is indissolubly bound up with His justice. Why Evil is permitted to exist at all, why it visits the righteous, this he is not told. Enough to know that all is well in the hands of its Creator. A higher answer is to be read by us in the light of the Sacrifice on Calvary, and of all that is involved in the mystery of the Cross.

Tortured as Job is at once by outward calamity and by inward distraction, feeling each upbraiding speech as a fresh wound, what wonder if his language is not wholly blameless, and if he is led on to utter some rash words, as he admits in his confession, "Wherefore I abhor myself and repent in dust and ashes." What wonder while he gropes after some support, if

> "oft his cogitations sink as low
> As, through the abysses of a joyless heart
> The heaviest plummet of despair can go?"

But not so. Still his faith remains unbroken, "Though he slay me, yet will I trust in him." Again and again does he call on the great Reader of hearts to witness that he is innocent of the sins so cruelly insinuated, and which he could not have admitted without hypocrisy.

And thus there comes the great controversy in which "God and man are brought face to face as it were in the desert." Thus it is that good is brought out of the machinations of Satan, and the shallow judgments of human ignorance. Thus the ways of God are justified to man.

Certainly there is much in this book to engage our attention and enlist our sympathy: much, too, I venture to think, that may check the restlessness and sober the thoughts of us "in these last days." Does it not speak to us calmly, dispassionately, but with intense earnestness, on the most absorbing topic that can occupy a rational being? the position in which he stands to his Maker?

Again, to glance at another portion of it: Has the mighty advance of Science, with all its latest discoveries in the world of Nature, and especially in its surprising additions to our knowledge of the heavenly bodies,—has all this detracted in the smallest degree from the sublimity and the truth of those majestic chapters in which God the Creator answers Job out of the whirlwind?[1] In statement and in form the book may be antiquated, but in spirit it will never grow old.

---

[1] "The attempt which is here made to group together the overwhelming marvels of nature, to employ them for the purpose of providing an approximate impression of the majesty of the Creator, though dependent upon the child-like, but at the same time deeply poetical, view of nature prevalent in antiquity, still retains not only its full poetical beauty, but also an imperishable religious worth. For though many of the phenomena here propounded as inexplicable, are referred by modern science to their proximate causes, and comprehended under the general laws of nature, yet these laws themselves, by their unalterable stability and potent operation only the more evoke our amazement, and will never cease to inspire the religious mind with adoring wonder of the infinite Power, Wisdom, and Love by which the individual laws, and forces, and elements are sustained and ruled."—DILLMANN, quoted by Driver, "Introduction to the Literature of the Old Testament," ch. ix.

And can we forget that it is the book whose language is interwoven with one of our most solemn and beautiful services? Can we forget that declaration of the sufferer's unfaltering and inextinguishable reliance on a Redeemer, however dimly descried, whom "his eyes shall behold" which greets the mourner at the churchyard gate wherever our English Prayer Book is used? Can we forget that simple yet venerable record of man's precarious existence, which again by the graveside, follows after the triumphant aspiration of St. Paul, and blends with that inspired message from the unseen world, "I heard a voice from heaven, saying unto me, Write, from henceforth blessed are the dead which die in the Lord, even so saith the Spirit, for they rest from their labours."

Strong are the claims which this Book has upon our reverence, and beyond this, it stands alone in Hebrew literature. Around it have gathered various questions of great interest as to the age to which it is to be referred, and the scene in which the story is laid, which cannot be adequately treated here.

But one of these should be perhaps mentioned; it is this. Is it after all only a parable? a weighty and solemn parable, indeed, but one that is wholly devoid of historical interest—a pure invention (an idea which was first broached in the Talmud) or does it describe a real character and actual events?

Probably the truth lies between the two extremes. It cannot be a literal history, for the dialogue is too subtle, too weighted with thought and argument, to have been extemporized; it is the result of leisure and reflection. Nor again is it entirely the work of the imagination; for Job is spoken of by Ezekiel as a real person, and since the author of the book writes as a teacher, he would have succeeded better by taking a popular character as his hero than one who was unfamiliar. But on neither view does the Book lose its value to us. Its moral teaching does not stand or fall with the literal accuracy of the details, any more than does the moral value of the parable of Dives and Lazarus depend upon the reality of the subjects of that aweful picture.

Or if we believe it to be in the main a product of creative genius, but resting on historical fact, having a basis of truth preserved by tradition (as was Luther's opinion) we need not be embarrassed. We need not perplex ourselves by trying to disentangle from the original tradition what is due to a later age. In either case it speaks to us as nothing less than the voice of God.

But you may say, I grant this story of one who lived and suffered long ago in a remote corner of the globe, is indeed deeply pathetic. It is, if you will, a mighty tragedy; but is it, you may ask, of any great value to us Christians?

I will endeavour to point out one or two ways in which it may be so, both generally and in the special warning of the text.

I. Never suffer yourselves to despise any human being however abject his lot, however degraded his condition. It is not unnecessary to remind *you* of this, enjoying as you do so largely the comforts of wealth, and liable as you are both here and in later life, when you will have great opportunities, to use it well, or to forget the poor with their slender store and their hard struggle for existence.

Worldly blessings come and go. Weighed in the balance against integrity of life, against purity of purpose, they are *absolutely as nothing*. That miserable man begging in the streets whom you feel tempted to pass by with scorn, has still something in him which demands respect. He bears the human form which Christ deigned to bear. He has an immortal spirit, for which Christ lived and died. We may dismiss him with the thought that perhaps he deserves his present state; but there is in him the possibility of restoration; at least we know not his trials in the past. We know not his scant measure of opportunity compared with our own. We cannot tell what may be in store for him hereafter.

Sometimes over the face of some miserable person, as the mists of wretchedness clear off, and the end is unmistakeably drawing near, there comes a dignity which it never wore before. This I have seen, and a new light has flashed upon those wondrous words: "Who shall change the body of our humiliation, that it may be fashioned like unto His glorious body."

I look upon Job in prosperity as the pattern priest and head of a family, who feels that there exists something far beyond earthly comfort, and recognizes its certain danger, its proneness to self-reliance, to softness, and to wantonness. Very touching is his anxiety for his sons, and the glimpse we have of his sanctifying them, and offering sacrifices for them after the days of their feasting: "For it may be," he said, "that my sons have sinned and cursed God in their hearts."

I look upon him again in adversity as a type of Him, to whom no shade of human misery was unfamiliar, in sympathy at least if not in actual experience, "whose lovers and friends were put away from him," who was "made perfect by suffering," who was "despised and rejected of men, smitten of God and afflicted . . . a man of sorrows and acquainted with grief."

II. Another lesson we may learn, I think, from this Book, is that the rule of duty is the best remedy for the perplexities of doubt. All paths of inquiry if pursued in a proper spirit will emerge at last into light, the light which shines down upon a well-spent life. "Man is born not to solve the problem of the universe (as has been well said), but to find out where the problem begins, and then to restrain himself within the limits of the comprehensible."[1] Everyone who reflects has some time or other been startled at the apparent inequalities of fortune; but even where the union of goodness and suffering is beyond all doubt, let nothing make us fret ourselves at this, or forget that we are in God's kingdom, and that all things work together for good to them that love Him. Many problems in life are difficult. The wisest cannot—need not attain to them; but there is one thing also most difficult to attain unto, and yet which we must strive to reach, and that is Heaven. And however dark may be the riddle of this painful world, we have light enough if we look

[1] "Goethe's Conversations with Eckermann," Oxenford's Translation, p. 161.

for it in the right direction, to guide our steps thither. "The sphere of active Duty is wide, sufficing, and ennobling."

> "Thou who art Victory and Law
> When empty terrors overawe;
> From vain temptations dost set free,
> And calm'st the weary strife of frail humanity."

Lastly, to follow this thought one step further and clothe it if possible in a definite form. Shun all you know to be dangerous. If Job could use the words of our text; if David, after saying in child-like simplicity (as he could before his great sin) "I have kept the ways of the Lord, I have an eye unto all his laws," could yet in the very next verse say, "*I eschewed mine own wickedness*," and thus recognize an inherent sinfulness, against which he had ever to be on his guard, who can feel himself safe? Whatever it be, lay your finger upon any one festering sore and bring it before the Great Physician. It may be something locked in the secret chamber of your own heart unknown to your dearest friend. It is surprising how the expulsion of any one noxious habit can purify the whole moral atmosphere of a man. One thorough act of self-searching, one calm prayer, one chapter or one psalm, read as if we were children listening to a loving father, one high and holy thought garnered and treasured up against temptation, oh, how much may even these accomplish!

And then think again how God must be offended by sin, provoked every day by it. "Such as be foolish shall not stand in Thy sight." It is only by His Holy Spirit working in our conscience that we can see the true nature of wrong acts. Oh suffer Him then to convince you now, so shall he not convict you eternally! "*Thou writest bitter things against me!*" Yes, there lies the true significance of sin, to which the heathen could never penetrate. It is not merely a missing the mark, a falling short of the highest ideal of beauty. It is not only depravity, *i.e.* a perversion of man's being; it is not only defilement—it is all this, but it is infinitely more. It is not mere discovering or branding by society that embitters it. "It is against thee, thee only that I have sinned and done this evil in thy sight."

I might dwell upon what it must be "to possess the iniquities of youth," upon their hampering and enfeebling effects, upon the shame inevitably caused before companions by the memories of a past made far less lovely than it might have been; upon the tears of parents; upon the terrible power gained over their victims by those who tempt and are listened to; upon the difficulty of breaking the fatal spell and escaping free from its influence. But I forbear to do so. Rather would I point to the strong stimulus, the sustaining support, the sweet comfort there is to be found in thoughts of good together done in boyhood; and to the special blessings promised to those who have set God always before them.

May Christ's precious atonement blot out the handwriting of anything that is against any one of us! May he take it out of the way and nail it to His Cross! May it never be yours to say, when you revisit Eton, "Thou writest bitter things against me."

And if memory will at times haunt us with the thought of "the iniquities of our youth,"—let us bear that pain meekly, as part of sin's penalty, remembering our old faults, not so as to give way to despair, but so as to abhor them more thoroughly, and trusting that at last this bitterness too will cease in that high world where there shall be no more curse, and therefore no more torturing recollections,—but where, when we wake up after God's likeness, we shall be satisfied with it, and shall hear His voice saying, "Behold I make all things new."

SERMON VIII.

LIGHT, NATURAL AND SPIRITUAL.[1]

"With thee is the well of life, and in thy light shall we see light."—*Psalm* xxxvi. 9.

WE may never know for certain the author of this Psalm, but we feel instinctively that the words are no mere human utterance. They recur again and again to the memory, like the cadence of some familiar music. Can we wonder that this verse was among St. Augustine's favourite passages? For it contains two great words, suggests two deep and wide subjects, *Life* and *Light*, God as the origin of Life, God as the source of Light. Under both of these images we remember that Christ has spoken of Himself, "I am the resurrection and the life,"—"I am the light of the world," and these two figures are combined by St. John in the opening of his Gospel, "In him was life, and the life was the light of men." How much, then, is wrapped up in these few words! To-day we will venture to

[1] February 6th, 1876.

speak but of one of these subjects, that contained in the latter part of the verse, "*In thy light shall we see light.*"

Let me ask you to pause and consider for a few minutes the marvellous nature of light.

How wonderful, may we not say how divine a thing it is! Few of us but must have felt this who have ever reflected about it at all. To the sick and weakly how cheering and invigorating; to the prisoner the only solace perhaps that he has, is the sunbeam glimmering through a crevice in his dungeon. And to all that are free and in health, after long periods of gloom, of dimness, and of depression, how does the glorious sun coming forth from his chamber restore the spirits, quicken the languid pulse, and add a fresh zest to existence. In the brief days of winter how we cherish its rays, and how eagerly, as the year proceeds, do we hail each indication that the hours of light are beginning to gain upon those of darkness! It is the absence of sunshine through nine dreary months that is the chief trial to those who have to winter in the arctic seas.

And what a world of hidden and forgotten life around us does it reanimate! For almost all life, indeed, light is a first necessity. It is true that animals can subsist for a time without it, but in most cases they soon lose health and pine away. It has been ascertained by the latest researches, that even at a vast depth the bed of the ocean contains a varied mass of animal existence. But still, it is of the very lowest type, and the creatures which tenant that dark abode, manifest scarcely any vital activity, while it would seem that no vegetation can thrive without some, though it be but ever so scanty a light. Below 100 fathoms a very rapid diminution of such life takes place. At the depth of 150 fathoms very few ordinary seaweeds are met with, and below this depth almost all traces of them disappear.

Think again of the vast space over which light has to travel, and at the same time of its rapidity. Fast as our planet sweeps along its orbit, Light travels about 10,000 times faster. Are not both of these facts marvellous? The enormous distances which it traverses while its transmission seems to us instantaneous,—and again, the enormous speed with which those distances are accomplished?

What wonder, then, if impressed only by the mere obvious properties of light, the greatest poets have dwelt upon it, have created images of new worlds by ideas and impressions with which it supplied them. It illuminates Dante's noble poem. Into his description of Paradise nothing gross or earthly is admitted. "Light, simple, unalloyed, unshadowed, eternal,

—never fails him as the expression of gradations of bliss."[1] And who can forget the words of Milton, "Hail holy light, offspring of heaven first born"? Written though they were twenty years after blindness had settled upon him, how exquisitely true are they! How full is his memory of the blessings of that "sovran vital lamp," how keen his sensibility to its power, and still how resigned is his prayer!

And yet little did *he* know of the wonders of light, compared with what was to be revealed. It was not till the year after Milton's death (1675) that Sir Isaac Newton published his discovery that white light is a compound,—a compound of many different colours. And since Newton's time, and more especially of late years, what a series of discoveries has there been! what astonishing truths have been established by gradual, by patient, by cautious observation! Think for a moment of the secret revealed by those coloured bands, the rainbow-tinted streak of the solar spectrum. That the delicate examination and minute mapping out of a ray of light passed through a prism, and of the dark lines which cross and break those bands of light,—that this should reveal the chemical constitution of our sun, millions of miles as it is removed from us,—

[1] Dean Church.

that it should be possible to assert the existence in its atmosphere of metals in a state of vapour, —might have seemed not long since the wildest of dreams. And yet this is only a part of what has been done. For the same principle has been extended to the stars. How amazing, then, is this great discovery! Those dark spaces and gaps are not the result of caprice, but of strict, unerring law. They point to particular rays which are absent, which have been arrested in their passage, and prove that the substance which gives out that kind of light is now burning in the sun. How truly has it been said, " A ray of light is a world in miniature ! "

These reflections but glance at the stupendous results of the investigations by which the astronomer has penetrated almost into the very laboratory of heat and light. The sole object had in view in making them, and which I trust will justify them in this place, is that they may lead us to consider with feelings of more and more reverence what must be the Author of Light,—what must be essential, original, underived Light, τὸ φῶς τὸ ἀληθινόν. "He that made the eye, shall not he see?" and He that spake the word,—the very first word, remember, that is recorded to have been pronounced, "*Let there be light!*" shall there be any darkness at all in Him? Shall it not be emphatically true that in Him, in the fullest and deepest sense, shall we see Light?

Let us then from this thought strive to carry home, each of us, something that may brighten our common days and seemingly prosaic cares, whether it be greater clearness and definiteness of vision in times of perplexity, or solace under affliction, or fresh strength and support to lift the burden from our heart and to raise us above our lower nature, whenever temper or passion, or self in any of its subtle forms would assert its dominion over us.

I. *In thy Light, O everlasting Father, shall we see Light.* "God *is* Light, says St. John, adding as is his manner when he would strengthen a statement—the denial of its opposite—" and in Him is no darkness at all." What means he by this? "In the material world, darkness is the absence of light; in the spiritual world darkness, that is, untruthfulness, deceit, falsehood, is the absence of God." For does not Light, of all things, most readily lend itself to such a figure, from its purity, from its beauty, from its life-sustaining properties? St. Paul can scarce find language to describe the desperate state of the Ephesians, so long as they were aliens, strangers having no hope, and without God in the world. Of the same Ephesians, when they had washed their robes, he says, "Now are ye light, walk

VIII] *Light, Natural and Spiritual.*

as children of the light." Yes, out of God all is, and must be, darkness. There may be a glitter, a delusive appearance, but it will fade away, it will not bear the test, if brought into contact with that holiness. Just as the brightest light that we can produce is as nothing to sunlight; so are all such specious imitations. There is a light (the limelight) so brilliant that we cannot look at it, any more than we can gaze unharmed at the sun. But if you place it in front of the sun, and look at it through a darkened glass, it is reduced to a black spot. So is it with man's most splendid triumphs. The highest intellectual enlightenment, the keenest human joy, the noblest achievements, the most fascinating society, what are they all when viewed in comparison with the intensity of Divine Light? And what is their worth in themselves, excepting so far as they partake of, and are confessed to depend upon it, as their sanction and their primal source?

Often in history has " an age of light, light without love, glared on the aching sight." The period preceding the preaching of Christianity was such an age. "Across the night of Paganism" it has been said, " Philosophy flitted on, like the lantern-fly of the tropics, a light to itself, and an ornament, but alas! no more than an ornament to the surrounding darkness." The error consisted in attempting to reach, and cleanse, and convert the heart through the understanding, instead of appealing in the first instance to the heart.

Have you not felt it to be true that all is darkness out of God? Once habituate yourself to rely upon your own unaided powers "to walk" (as Isaiah says) "in the light of your fire, and in the sparks that you have kindled," to use His name lightly, to sneer at holy things, to trifle with daily prayer, to harbour the thought that this delightful life of yours is not God's gift, or rather a precious trust to be demanded with interest, but yours to use or abuse, to ennoble or degrade as you think fit, and do not the avenues of light become stopped and clogged from that moment? O beware, I pray you, lest without His rays streaming in upon your soul to enlighten it, it remains—as it must then remain —a confused chaos of wayward propensities. "If the light that is in thee be darkness, how great is that darkness!"

II. *In thy Light, O Christ, shall we see light.* How hopeless, how impossible, to have light apart from Him, in whom "dwelleth all the fulness of the Godhead bodily!" All that was best and loftiest in the utterances of the sages of old, was due to the true Light, which lighteth every man that cometh into the world. He is "the express image of the Father," no mere reflection, but standing in the same relation to Him as does the sunlight to the sun. By filling ourselves with the effulgence that streams from His life on earth, His intensity of love and self-sacrifice, His sweetness and His strength, we shall draw in light that will reach beyond the region of the heart. The eyes of the understanding also will be opened to welcome the truth. We shall no longer wander away into the dusky wilderness of sin, wherever the *ignis fatuus* of our own fancies and follies chance to lead us. Each day will be felt more and more to be stamping us whose we are, and reminding us to whom we should consecrate every faculty we possess, every blessing we enjoy, every trial it may be good for us to undergo.

III. *In thy Light, O Holy Ghost, the Comforter, shall we see light.* Can it be that any true insight, any abiding influence for good shall exist apart from Him? Think of the prayer in the Confirmation Service, for His sevenfold gifts! Through Him you will be enabled, not only to walk in the Light, but to be centres of Light to others. Few minds, one has said, are sunlike, even among the best. The generality are content to absorb light, without reflecting it. To be eager to be illuminated, to resolve not to be left to our own phantoms, this is, indeed, a great step. But it is not all. All the grandest types of character, prophets and saints like Elijah, and John the Baptist, and St. Paul, or like Anselm and Bernard in mediæval times, have been such sources of light to the world around them. And though few can rival them, still all in their degree may strive to burn like lamps; to shine with steady rays from the heaven of noble thoughts, and the serenity of calm and well-spent lives.

Were it not well to set before yourselves such an ideal; to be fired with such an ambition *now*, while you are young? Not to dim and enfeeble, but to brighten and hand on brighter to others, the original light within you?

Believe me there are very many ways in which this is possible.

First, there is the Lamp of Intelligence, of clear and piercing insight, which sees things as they really are, and calls things by their true names; which will not knowingly be misled, or lured on into what is questionable; which can set its proper value upon what is fleeting, as compared with what is abiding and precious. This gift of an unclouded vision is the privilege of all in early youth. But it is a birthright far too often forfeited and lightly esteemed. This Lamp, if you are careful to trim it, and nourish it with all that is healthy in what you see and read and meditate upon; if you guard it from being extinguished by violent gusts of appetite or passion, if you pray God daily to keep it fresh and undimmed, this Lamp of Intelligence, and of a right judgment in all things will enable you not only to steer your own bark, but to help others to shape their course aright. You will see the dangers that beset them; you will speak a good word in season; you will not look on with neglect and indifference, whilst they drift on helplessly upon the rocks and shoals, which you may have escaped, but by which their young life is still encompassed.

Then again, there is the Lamp of Learning: the thirst for knowledge, the desire to have a firm grasp and possession of some one portion, whatever it be, and be it ever so small, of the vast and ever-increasing field of science. This is a lamp, which here at least ought never to be in danger of being extinguished. In pursuing this, our central aim, let all of us work together. How much we can all of us learn from each other! pupils from the experience of tutors; tutors from the daily sight of and intercourse with boyhood, gaining sympathy with its struggles, interest in its pursuits, and elasticity and fresh vigour for their work!

And there is a third way in which we may both see the light, and be centres of light to others. I mean the Lamp of Holiness, of an innocent and unstained life. Whatever else we study, let us study "holiness, without which no man shall see the Lord." This is absolutely necessary for any genuine light. The Lamp of Learning will burn but faintly and feebly if it be not fed by daily prayer to God that He may sanctify it with His Spirit:

"Let knowledge grow from more to more,
But more of reverence in us dwell."

One of the most profound scholars of the seventeenth century, Casaubon, never began his morning labours without first studying the Scriptures, and never closes the record of his daily work without thankfulness for having accomplished what he had done ($\sigma \grave{\upsilon} \nu\ \Theta \epsilon \tilde{\omega}$). This is within the reach of all. Genius, great accomplishments, high place in the world, may or may not be yours. But all, if they strive earnestly after them, can aim at moral courage, at gentleness, at sincerity, at guilelessness, without a misgiving that their efforts will prove utterly vain.

One further characteristic of this lamp is, that it glows, with an ever-increasing brightness, in those who value and cherish it. Have you not felt, after some more than ordinarily severe struggle with yourself, after communing with your own heart and in your chamber, that times of refreshing, times of illumination have come, and that you have been able to say and feel as you have never said or felt before, *With thee is the well of life, and in Thy Light have I seen light?*

Pray then for this heavenly guidance more and more! Feel that you must go forth to do battle with your foes, arrayed in a panoply of divinely-wrought armour, and with a radiant light upon your head, kindled by no human hand. Feed your Lamp with the oil of prayer, and well-directed study of the Sacred Volume.

"Thy word is a lamp unto my feet and a light unto my path." To revert for a moment to those wonderful discoveries of our times: if by intense and patient examination of those lines in the solar ray fresh knowledge is being every day wrested from the far-off realms of space, so by reading the highest page of revelation, may not we too penetrate nearer into the secret of Christ's life, and see what we must be, if we would be like Him, as He bids us be?

Yes! We must become like him. Let us ask ourselves in all seriousness, Am I trying in any degree to reflect in my own mind the mind which was in Christ Jesus? Am I surprised, startled, ashamed, to feel at times how very unlike Him I am? Do I suffer any counterfeit religion to pass current for His Word? Am I very watchful lest by dallying with what is doubtful in thought, or fatal in act, by letting the little cloud of any one pernicious habit rise above the horizon and gather silent force, the soul's fair sunshine may become (as too surely it will then become) darkened and overcast?

It is with a fine perception of the truth, that only by the spiritually-minded can spiritual things be discerned, that Tennyson has described the various fortunes of those knights who rashly vowed they would go in search of the Holy Grail. Alas! they had not counted the cost when they sallied forth into the wilderness. How many of them followed wandering fires, and were lost in quagmires! How few returned—scarce a tithe—of that goodly company, weary and faint and footsore, confessing sorrowfully that the quest was not for them. For one knight alone was the mystic vision reserved. Yes! so it is, and ever will be. To Isaiah, to Ezekiel, to the aged apostle in Patmos, to such as can lose themselves to save themselves—who live, even here, in an element of heaven, and even here can catch its melodies—whose senses are quickened, and whose mortal armour is transfigured and made light, to such as these is it granted to pierce behind the veil. In Thy light shall he see light, whose heart is pure, whose example is a daily comfort and encouragement to his friends, whose path shineth more and more unto the perfect day, because he humbly and steadfastly pursues to the end the one fixed goal. Of him, when at last the shadows seem, but only seem, to close around him (for he is passing from shadows to substance) of him can it be confidently said,

> "Oh, just and faithful knight of God!
> Ride on! the prize is near!"

SERMON IX.

THE REGULATION OF THOUGHTS.[1]

"Try me, O God, and seek the ground of my heart: prove me, and examine my thoughts."—*Psalm* cxxxix. 23.

EXAMINE my thoughts, O God! How few of us here really desire that! How few would endure such an ordeal! And this, whatever we understand by *thought*, whether we take it in its stricter sense, as the faculty in us by which we reflect, compare, and reason; or whether we employ the word in its wider and larger sense of the whole region of the mind, so as to include what the Bible calls "the imaginations of the heart," all those devices, notions, purposes, which we are so constantly forming.

When we pause, and turn our gaze inward upon our thoughts (using the word as we will do in its broader and scriptural sense), may we not well be filled with wonder at what they reveal, and almost with despair at what the regulation of them involves? These thoughts

[1] October 5th, 1879.

of ours (are we not sometimes tempted to say?) so impalpable, so fugitive, so evanescent, one flash of which often imperils our best purposes; how are we to command them? For word and act we are responsible, but can we be accountable for what seems to come and go independent of our own will? Shall we *really* be judged for these hereafter?

Think what stages there are in the growth and history of a single mind. Think, alas! by what gusts of passion it is swayed! To what stagnation it is reduced by sloth or by the predominance of the sensual element. What a paralysis comes over it at times, perhaps for long intervals, through neglect, and lethargy, through frivolous and unworthy habits! What breaks and chasms there are in the plans and projects of even the noblest minds! some of them being abandoned, others taken up in their place—mere sketches and outlines! how many are begun and never carried out—unravelled at the end of a month or a year, like the fabled web that seemed destined never to be completed.

Or, think again of all those roving, restless imaginations, that interrupt the steady course of thought! those unbidden and unwelcome guests that will insist on being with us—those visionary schemes, in which we are too apt to indulge—that are so resolutely intrusive, that will invade the chambers of memory, and will make us listen to their appeal.

Nevertheless, in spite of (or rather in consequence of all this), we must study to curb and control our own thoughts. "God shall bring every work into judgment, with every secret thing, whether it be good or whether it be evil."[1] He understandeth our thoughts long before. He can, and if we earnestly pray Him to do so, He will, cleanse them by the inspiration of His Holy Spirit.

This duty is emphatically a Christian duty. Not that there are not some traces of it in heathen philosophies, besides several enforcements of it in the Old Testament. To take one heathen instance, the Emperor Marcus Aurelius says, in those "Meditations" (composed in hours snatched from the labours of the camp): "Since it is possible that thou mayest depart from life this very moment, regulate every act and every thought accordingly!" and again, "Such as are thy habitual thoughts, such also will be the character of thy mind, for the Soul is dyed by the thought."

If we open the Psalter we find many a warning that the region of thought is a dangerous region. "O let not mine heart be inclined to any evil thing." "Let (not merely) the words of my mouth but also the medita-

[1] Eccles. xii. 14.

tions of my heart be always acceptable in thy sight!" "Thou requirest truth in the inward parts." "Make me a clean heart, O God, and renew a right spirit within me!"

Specially is this brought out in this marvellous 139th psalm. The key-note is God's omniscience: "O Lord thou hast searched me out and known me. Thou understandest my thoughts long before." Clear and manifest to His scrutiny are their hidden workings; as too, were the mysterious beginnings of life itself, its yet undeveloped course, its thread rolled as it were in a ball, to be unwound as days pass on. All was fashioned by Him, and it is to Him that the psalmist, overwhelmed by such a presence, lifts the concluding prayer, "Try me, O God, and seek the ground of my heart. Prove me and examine my thoughts."

But still more brightly does this truth shine forth from the gospel page. Christ claims to be Lord of the Christian's innermost being. He penetrates to the very depths of the human heart. His word is "a discerner of the thoughts and intents." Could it be otherwise with Him who pierced through the hypocrisy of Scribe and Pharisee, who read the unuttered reasonings of the twelve, as to which of them should be the greatest? Could He fail to claim the allegiance of those parts of our nature which constitute the springs of character? He to whom Peter exclaimed, "Lord, thou knowest all things, thou knowest that I love thee." He, whose whole Sermon on the Mount proposes the highest ideal of inward holiness, and insists upon the single eye, the entire unselfishness of motive, the strictest purity of imagination?

Now if Christ "knew what was in man" He would not surely demand of him anything beyond his powers. How far then, let us ask, can we command these thoughts of ours over which He asserts such an intense, such an absolute hold?

First, we can largely influence them through *Memory* and its two great aids *Attention* and *Association*. Original differences in the power of memory will always exist in different minds; still the excuse we are so prone to plead of bad memory, generally means feeble attention. Without intense direction of the mind to what is before it, there can be no distinct recollection. And this is equally true, is it not, of religious thought? Nor let us forget how our Saviour enforces this, " He that hath ears to hear, let him hear."

And then even more powerful is that familiar law of the *Association of Ideas*. Contemplate two or more facts or notions together, or in immediate succession, and they will soon become so connected that one of them at a future time is sure to recall the other. Contemplate them frequently and attentively, and a train of ideas, without any mental effort, will follow in a more and more strong and steady current. Of what infinite importance then is correct association; for as surely as men do not "gather grapes of thorns or figs of thistles," so surely will impure, envious, sordid, unfeeling thoughts — the fatal outcome of ideas wrongly associated—bring forth a rank and grievous crop of evil living, a woe for future years.

This, then, is the *first* power we each possess over our thoughts (and is it, I would ask, anywhere more vital, more influential, than here among you?) the germ of childhood's crudest notions, the key to much of the history of youth, the basis of a large part of the habits of maturer age—this noble, this perilous, this mysterious faculty of association.

But secondly, we can *select* from our thoughts and we can reject. "We can arrest these noiseless travellers (as they have been called) in their course, and question them as to their ultimate destination."[1] We can select the healthy. "Whatsoever things are true, whatsoever things are worthy of respect and rever-

[1] Sermons by T. Grant, 1812.

ence, whatsoever things are just, whatsoever things are pure, whatsoever things are lovely, whatsoever things are of good report."[1]

These things, rather than their deadly opposites, we càn think of if we care to make the effort. Or we can, alas, put sweet for bitter, and bitter for sweet.

Think how we employ this power every day of our lives, how we can change and divert the stream of images and recollections. When we refer to a book or the index of a book for a special object, we find it possible, do we not, to keep out irrelevant thoughts, and to refuse to entertain all but the particular one for which we opened it. We force the mind in this case into an opposite channel to that which it would spontaneously take. We direct it whither we would. Oh, then, let us direct it and force it in other cases! If we can choose whether we will embrace and cherish evil imaginations as they arise, or strangle them at their birth, if we can bid them welcome or bid them "avaunt," shall we not say to our souls, "How long shall thy vain thoughts lodge within thee?"[2] Shall we not in their place treasure up the holy text, the ejaculatory prayer, the heroic ideal, and have them ready for use as antidotes against the poison of temptation?

[1] Phil. iv. 8.   [2] Jer. iv. 14.

And then, again, we can *concentrate* our thoughts. We can turn a deaf ear to wandering digressions and chance solicitations. Without this how would anything great be ever written? How would anything difficult ever be achieved? Has not the historian to throw himself heart and soul into past ages; has he not to live in them, as it were, if he would give us a vivid picture of them? Yes, precious is this gift of concentration, never perhaps more needed than now. As precious as its opposite is worthless; that desultory habit of mind which skims the surface of many subjects, never settling on any one; without sustained effort, without method, or definiteness of aim.

But thirdly, we can further *discipline* our thoughts. We can review and marshal them by self-observation. Man not only has the prerogative of reflecting upon things outside him, but he can turn his gaze upon the phenomena of his inner being. And he must do so. For, consider, what a capacity for good or evil there is in his heart! "It is Pandora's box,"[1] says an old writer, "which lets fly innumerable plagues and mischiefs." "It is a noisy inn or hostelry full of turmoil, with fresh arrivals and departures every instant,

---

[1] Chilcot, "Evil Thoughts," 1698.

every passing thought seeking admittance." Conversation, books, friendships, habits, open a thousand avenues to it. What is to reduce it to harmony with itself and with all around it? What, indeed, but constant *recollectedness*, constant challenging of our thoughts and sentiments, making them "give up their passports," constant bearing in mind the One great Reader of Thoughts?

All this (you will say) is very easy in theory and on paper. It is one thing to map out the region, it is a very different thing to conquer it, and establish firm dominion over it. "Who is sufficient for these things?" It is, indeed, difficult to control our thoughts. It belongs to the highest branch of self-discipline. It cannot be gained at once. The deep-seated tendencies of each man and each boy's nature are not to be made light of. Often there are two opposing forces to be met. We have the tendency of the *mind* to flow in the direction of the strongest association, to cherish one class of thought. We have also the *feelings* influencing the thoughts. But the difficult is not the impossible. By patient training where the disposition is weak, by sterner force used on ourselves where passion is strong and thought rebellious, by perseverance, by self-knowledge, by self-distrust, by prayer to God the Father that He will not leave His children to drift without a rudder to the mind He has implanted in them; by prayer to Christ and His Holy Spirit that They will reduce to order whatever is turbulent in us; by sedulous avoidance of all we know to be dangerous, gradually, if not at once, we can stem the vehement flood of our unruly imaginations.

Let me, then, with all earnestness endeavour by a few suggestions to press home to you this vital subject of which we have touched, as it were, but the fringe.

First, let your thoughts be real. Let them, as far as can be, be genuinely your own. Let them be steadily and distinctly thought out. Where exactness is required direct the mind in all its intensity to what is before it. Grapple with the difficult problem, return to it, leave it not till it have yielded up its secret. Never let us give way to a listless inactive habit of mind. If we echo the sentiments of others, let us do so because we have really meditated over them and are convinced of their truth. This vigorous tension of the faculties will reach, believe me, beyond the sphere of mental acquirements. It will give sincerity and stability to your whole life. It will go to build up the character of the man, who, "whatsoever his hand findeth to do, doeth it with his might."

And, next, dwell frequently on what is exalted and elevated. Let there be chambers in your mind where, despite of all that is seemingly prosaic in life, noble images may remain enshrined. Our studies here would indeed be open to exception did they not aim at fixing our attention on the loftiest ideals in legend, in history, in poetry. Treasure up those truths that wake to perish never. If in what you read in private, you habitually breathe an unwholesome atmosphere; if you dwell upon what you know by experience will impair the energy and dull the brightness of the mind by its paltriness and emptiness, even if it does not positively corrupt it ; or, again, if we wilfully harbour the uncharitable thought that rests upon slender or upon no foundation, how then can we honestly say, " *Lead me not into temptation*"? Still, at the same time, thirdly, let our thoughts be sober and orderly. Retaining the ardour of enthusiasm, it is good also for young men to be sober-minded. Ask yourselves after the excitement of each day, *What have been my prevailing thoughts this day?* What is their general colour and tone? Are they roving, restless, unsatisfied? What do I most think of; and why do I think of it? This characteristic of order is seen in all great minds. It was a marked feature in James Watt, the improver of the steam engine, so much so that "he could reject instinctively everything immaterial. Every notion suggested to him seemed instantly to take its proper place among the other rich furniture of his mind."

But once more, it is much that our thoughts be real, free from all hypocrisy and affectation; it is much that they be lofty, free from all that is sordid; it is much that they be orderly. But it is not all. They must also be *holy*.

There *is* a sense in which God can be in *all* our thoughts; and we can bring into captivity *every* imagination to the obedience of Christ, that He may keep ward over them, as in a strong fortress; not, of course, that direct, continuous meditation on exclusively sacred subjects is meant. Only let the remembrance of Him who is "about your path and about your bed" so pervade your life, that you may say from your heart, "the darkness is no darkness with Thee," and that you may feel at rising, 'When I wake up I am present with Thee."

Alas! must not some of us confess that so far from seeking God's kingdom, the question has been, How can I crowd the greatest amount of pleasure, perhaps of dangerous pleasure, into this day? Doubtless there will be times when we have less glow and fervour. There are "tides of the spirit" and of the higher energies. Still throughout the day keep some holy text not far from the memory—"Thou, O God, seest me." How can I do—how can I even imagine—this wickedness?

Say not, It was a mere thought. Remember "the greatest sin ever committed was at first but a thought."[1] That wild fancy, if fostered, is the germ of you know not what misery. Those unhallowed thoughts, dally not with them! Dream not of conquering them unaided! Go at once to Him who can dry up the tainted current at the fountain head! And above all, specially within these walls, surrender to Him the entire domain of your inner being. Recollect that strong, but not too strong, description of the guilty king, and his fruitless attempt to pray:

> "My words fly up, my thoughts remain below:
> Words, without thoughts, never to Heaven go."[2]

And now this evening—to clothe in an outward practical form these laws of mind on which we have been dwelling—I call on you to link the thought of your own health and happiness with the thought of the sickness and suffering of others. Your alms are asked for the Windsor and Eton Infirmary. Many of you, it may be, the mere force of contrast will influence to help towards supporting and furthering its good work. But may it not be with some here that there is the association of personal experience? Some of you

---

[1] Chilcot, *ut supra*.
[2] "Hamlet," act iii., sc. 3.

have known, have you not, what the hours are spent in the sick chamber? how slow they pass, how monotonous they seem, how helpless they make you feel, and how dependent upon the thoughtfulness, the kindness, the gentle ministrations of others?

And if *you*, with all the tenderest care and all the surroundings of wealth have felt this, how much more those for whom we plead! Set their want against your plenty; set their feebleness against your buoyant strength; set their confinement against your ample liberty of girding yourselves and walking whither you would! Oh; think how much of Christ's work on earth was devoted to visiting, comforting, and healing those in bodily pain! The very name of hospital existed not—for the thing did not exist—before He came.

I know few sights more touching than the one that can be witnessed from that bridge in London, where, facing England's great council chambers, stands that series of buildings, with its terraces, on which you may sometimes discern the pale, weary, emaciated forms of a few poor convalescents, able once more to refresh and gladden themselves with the blessed air and light of heaven. The river beneath them, with its alternate current, gives only too apt an emblem of the ebb and flow in the precarious lives of those poor sufferers.

It is such an institution—one near us—that appeals to you this evening. Oh! if you have of late been strengthened and exhilarated, if your pulses have beat high with the full current of healthy exercise, on moor or mountain; if nobler thoughts and aspirations have sprung up in you, sailing over some rock-girt loch, or gazing up some Alpine height; recollect those less fortunate ones who meantime have had patiently to endure, to hope against hope, to resign themselves perhaps to the certainty of no distant departure. Cut off some superfluous extravagance, some wasteful habit! Seize gladly this opportunity! Surely here, if anywhere, those lines are true :

> "Largely Thou givest, gracious Lord,
> Largely Thy gifts should be restor'd ;
> Freely Thou givest, and Thy word
>   Is 'Freely give.'
> He only, who forgets to hoard,
>   Has learn'd to live."

Sermon X.

THE MISUSE OF WORDS: PERVERSION OF LANGUAGE.[1]

"The vile person shall be no more called liberal nor the churl said to be bountiful."—*Isaiah*, xxxii. 5.

OF what blest period in the history of the human race is the Prophet Isaiah here speaking? Of what golden age when "Truth shall flourish out of the earth and righteousness look down from heaven," is this the description? When will this and all the other glowing language of this chapter be realized? Never in our own time. Never can we hope to see the vision fulfilled, literally, perfectly, and universally. It were vain to look for the supreme and absolute triumph of truth, until that time when Satan shall no longer be permitted to go forth and deceive the nations; until, in the words of the Litany, he is finally beaten down under our feet. Still, is there not, brethren, a sense in which we may recognize the truth of the text as belonging in part to the present state of

[1] September 25th, 1881.

existence? Is it not for each of us, in our own measure, to hasten on and further its accomplishment? Is it not our duty to do so? Is it not what we really mean, when day by day we breathe the prayer, or raise the hymn, "*Thy Kingdom come, O Lord*"?

Isaiah himself lived to witness a partial fulfilment of his own prediction. Under the government of a good king like Hezekiah, princes and magistrates did rule in judgment and execute their office with integrity and righteousness. He by his example and by the deliverance granted in his day, was for a time a refuge to his people, and "a covert from the tempest" of Assyrian invasion, when the "blast of the terrible ones was as a storm against the wall." But the sublime tone and the scope of these chapters refuse to be satisfied by such an inadequate account of their meaning. We may not imprison the heavenly spirit of prophecy within the earthly vessels of such interpretations. The vista of increasing happiness down which Isaiah gazed reached out far into the distant ages. He does but glance at the reign of the King of Judah, and the deliverance it conferred. They are but passing illustrations, shadows and images of the reign of Messiah; of the gradual but certain triumph of the Gospel, and of "that far-off Divine event to which the whole

Creation moves," that crowning consummation, when "the kingdoms of this world shall have become the kingdoms of our Lord and of his Christ."

What privilege can be higher than to promote the coming of that Kingdom, the dawn of that day when Christ shall at last have "put all enemies under his feet"? And of that blest time, of that perfect state, of that better land, there is one unmistakable characteristic (the only one on which we can dwell to-day), and that is the one given in our text.

There shall be a reversal of wrong judgments, a rectification, a setting right, a final and supreme readjustment, that shall strike conviction home at once to every mind and to every conscience, and from which there shall thenceforth be no possibility of appeal. Darkness shall no more be confounded with light, nor light with darkness. Sweet shall no longer be put for bitter, nor bitter for sweet. Evil men and evil opinions shall no longer be preferred to good men and good opinions. Doubtful or seemingly doubtful actions shall no longer be veiled under the superficial varnish of specious terms. They will be seen as they are in their essential nature. Doubt itself will vanish from that Kingdom, and be absorbed in the piercing light of truth; for 'all things are naked and opened unto the eyes of him with whom we have to do." "Eripitur persona manet res." The mask will be torn off, the reality will be left. Names shall correspond to things. "The vile person shall no longer be called liberal, nor the churl said to be bountiful."

The value of names, the danger of being misled by erroneous estimates—this I would endeavour to put briefly before you this evening, as I believe it to be of the utmost importance to us all.

> "O purblind race of miserable men,
> How many among us at this very hour
> Do forge a life-long trouble for ourselves,
> By taking true for false, or false for true;
> Here, thro' the feeble twilight of this world
> Groping, how many, until we pass and reach
> That other, where we see as we are seen!"

In no society, perhaps, does the power—might one not say the tyranny—of words exercise so powerful and so vital an influence, as it does here. Nowhere else, probably, can a word, according as it is rightly or wrongly applied, stamp upon a person, upon an institution, upon a custom so abiding a character. Nowhere else are words so readily caught up, or so eagerly repeated, or employed in so direct and plain a manner, and in terms so broad and unqualified, whether it be for praise or dispraise, as here in the large liberty of unrestricted intercourse which the members of a public school enjoy.

The judgments of the young often, like well-directed arrows, go straight to the mark; straighter, it may be, at times than even those of the older, if the mind has become warped and perverted by misleading prejudices of later years. This much we may admit, when they dart forth from a generous and unbiassed understanding, in simple cases of right and wrong, where neither their own personal interest, nor that of their companions, is at stake. But beyond this, do they not often need most serious qualification and correction? Are they not as frequently judgments that require to be again and again informed? Is not a little deeper insight destined to reverse them? You begin to see this as school-life draws to a close. You will see it more clearly when you have left us. But in the meantime the seed which has been scattered broadcast in the rash and indiscriminate judgment of earlier years is left to germinate in the minds of others. The light estimate of sins against purity, the half-profane jest, the facile designation that stereotypes some pernicious custom, the flimsy excuse that veils some dereliction of daily work, the perversions of language by which those who make a bold stand for duty are misrepresented, all 'these are instances of the abuse of words which often, alas, outlives their author. They are propagated in one form or another. They do not lose strength or vitality for want of fresh material. They grow steadily into a tradition, and that tradition may live on to mislead many a future generation.

My dear friends, in touching on the false estimates of character, which we are all so prone to make, let me ask you to pause and ponder with me the solemn truth that there is One who has sounded every depth of the human heart, and every variety of human character, and who reads each one of us here present this day exactly as he is, with infinite mercy and compassion, " with larger, other eyes than ours to make allowance for us all," yet at the same time (let us remember) with infinite truth, holding the balance with unswerving exactitude, because He, and He only, is the great reader of hearts, to whom all secrets are open. What if He were to describe us at this moment by the precise term, the proper epithet which suits our character? What are all *our* judgments which we pass so glibly and so unhesitatingly upon each other, when we think of that? How paltry, how insufficient, how one-sided! "Such as are foolish cannot stand" in the light of His scrutinizing and unerring gaze. The vile person, that is the *Nabal*, the fool, who has raised himself by successful scheming—before Him is not the *Nadib*, the Prince, the gentleman (such is the force of the original) however much he may pass muster as such with the world that looks only on the surface. The *churl*, however much he may veil his nature, and be courted, and caressed, and flattered, is seen by Him in his true colours. The proud Dives of this life (in the fine language of St. Augustine [1]) is the beggar of Hades. *Superbus temporis mendicus inferni.*

And so we are assured throughout the Bible that God is no respecter of persons; that is, He regards not the exterior semblance, but pierces to the inner reality. You recollect how He chose David, and took him away from the sheepfolds — how his seven brethren passed each before Samuel, and how when the prophet fancied that surely now the Lord's anointed was before him, he was undeceived. "Look not on his countenance or on the height of his stature ... for man looketh on the outward appearance, but the Lord looketh on the heart."

And do we not often misjudge those around us? Does not the open free-handedness of a boy who is somewhat richer than his com-

[1] Sermon CIII. on Luke, x. 16, "Qui vos spernit, me spernit."

panions, veil from their view the less striking but not less real liberality of another, who possesses in a larger measure the elements of true generosity? Do we never allow fluent readiness and cleverness to weigh with us above more sterling, though less dazzling qualities? Those, too, who have higher aims, and who do not catch at mere fleeting popularity, are exposed to errors in *their* judgments. The pride of culture and refinement is apt to look down on the illiterate and the backward,—to pronounce them hopeless, and to depreciate the good there is in those whose characters are cast in a different mould to their own.

Again, how easy it is to read amiss actions and motives of others! This is shown by the way in which time and circumstances modify our once so confident assertions. After the lapse of a few years, with the larger opportunities they have given us for forming our opinion, how different is our verdict! Have we not to confess that the fault lay in ourselves? in some dulness of perception, some readiness to acquiesce too hastily in popular judgments? some want of delicate appreciation, some failure to discriminate, that hurried us on to *label*, and to label wrongly with the title of vile or liberal, a character which as yet we had but dimly deciphered? And then how frequently does suffering or death come in to correct our judgments! *Too late* is inscribed upon much of human estimate. How often are we forced to soften down the sentence we used to pass upon our friend! Now that he is removed from us, we see to how much good we were blind during his lifetime. How bitterly do we regret the stinted measure of acknowledgment we yielded to his merits while he lived so near us! Such are some of the obvious dangers to which we are exposed in reviewing the actions and the motives of others.

What, then, is to be our rule? Is it not the divine one, "*Judge not that ye be not judged, condemn not that ye be not condemned*"? Is it not to suspend the hasty decision, and to check the too impulsive language, even it may be to keep silence at times, unless we are plainly and unmistakably called upon to speak out, where some broad principle of right and wrong is at stake, and where conscience can utter her decision in no faltering accents? Such occasions there may and must be. But in all cases let what we say be seasoned with the charity that thinketh no evil. In all cases, let our aim be to "judge not according to the appearance but to judge righteous judgment," and divert conversation away from the turbid channels in which it is so apt to run—the faults and foibles of our friend; to strive to hurt him, no, not by word, any more than by deed; to think,—*what if he knew all my secret life,*—my inner weakness? How humbling and sobering is that thought! How mercifully is the veil drawn! Oh! if he knew all, how could we bear it?

Let us then be more vigilant over words. "Care over them is the very secret and key of care over the whole life." " If any man offend not in word " (says St. James) " the same is a perfect man, and able also to bridle the whole body." Let us treasure our Saviour's warnings. " Every idle word which men shall speak, they shall give account thereof in the day of judgment." Not words, of course, of innocent recreation, nor words which sparkle with real wit and wisdom, but vapid, frivolous, unedifying, unfruitful words. Be sure that they are the beginning of half the hollowness and faithlessness and waste there is in the world. Let us call things by their right names, and not be deluded by the abuse of speech, as were the men of Isaiah's time, and as far too many are in our own day.

Never has the inner meaning of language been more laid open than by the researches into its origin made in our own time. By the language of a nation the rise and fall of its moral life may be indicated. Some of you will remember that striking chapter in which the Greek historian dwells upon the deadly bitterness of party spirit, and notes as one special symptom of it, that men "changed the accepted signification of words in their reference to action, by the way in which they thought proper to look at them."[1] Courage and rashness, prudence and cunning changed places in their vocabulary. Thus did they undermine the very foundations of society.

And the language in which he wrote contained one most expressive term[2] for the baneful alteration in the value of common words denoting blame or praise,—whether it be for the disparagement of the good, or for the glozing over and palliating the evil.

Oh, may God teach us *so* to use the blessing of speech that He has given us, as never to abuse it! may He grant to His minister that no weakness of his may impair the message he should deliver! When next we are tempted to err by random or hasty utterances, let us think of the Recording Angel, ready with his iron pen to write down on the indelible tablets what we shall vainly wish to recall. Let us refrain our lips and be more swift to hear, more slow to speak. And if ever we are being imposed upon by the fallacies of language, let us return again and again to Him

---

[1] Thucydides, iii. 82.
[2] ὑποκορίζεσθαι.

"who spake as never man spake," in "whose mouth was found no guile," and let us believe that, as He is Himself the Truth, so can He impart to all who ask of Him all the healing virtue of "the words of eternal life."

Sermon XI.

THE RECOVERY OF HEZEKIAH.[1]

"I have heard thy prayer, I have seen thy tears: behold, I will add unto thy days fifteen years."—*Isaiah*, xxxviii. 5.

SUCH was the message Isaiah was bidden to carry back to King Hezekiah when sick unto death; sick, that is, of a malady which in the natural course of things must have proved fatal. The command had gone forth: "Set thine house in order, for thou shalt die and not live." And then came the brighter vision granted to the Prophet, even before he had passed forth from the precincts of the palace; and these gracious words conveying the assurance of the reprieve, and the rapid recovery within three days.

Fifteen years! how insignificant a period when compared with those mighty revolutions of time in which Providence works; with the progress of the human race, or the history of a single nation: how long, on the other hand, in the retrospect, and still more in the prospect,

[1] April 29th, 1883.

of an individual's existence: "grande mortalis ævi spatium;" a large portion of human life, as the historian Tacitus calls this identical space of time, when touching upon his own career. How much does it comprise in its outward events, whether mournful or joyful; changes of fortune or circumstances, losses and gains, bereavements and blessings, and in God's *inward* dealings with the undying conscience, in the momentous lessons of the spirit's experience, how coloured is it with far deeper hues! If we look back with any seriousness with what a voice must the retrospect of fifteen years speak to us! How plainly do they tell us not to rely upon our life here (all important as are its uses and its issues). How do they bid us regard it as a mere atom in comparison with our whole, our higher being? How do they whisper to us that it is self-surrender, not self-seeking that will win us victory at last? If we look forward, which of us can venture to forecast the years? or to presume that fifteen years, or anything like such a period may be granted to us? and if it should so be, which of us can look onward without a wholesome dread borne in upon him by the lessons of the past? or without earnest prayer for that guiding Hand, without which, what we deem strength may prove in the day of trial to be but the most miserable weakness?

Fifteen years! Would this boon turn out to be an unmixed blessing? Was it likely to prove so in the instance before us? Was it in fact and in the result a real gain to the prostrate and passionate sufferer? Who shall venture to decide whether the prolongation of any given life by such an extension (an extension of more than a fifth of the Psalmist's limitation of human life) would or would not be desirable?

Let us dwell (1) On some features in the history of Hezekiah; (2) his prayer for length of days; (3) the answer to that prayer, and the sequel of his recovery.

What then is the general impression left on us by the life of this monarch from first to last? Is it not of one who had a lofty ideal, but united to it some weakness of character? Of one profoundly stirred by the grandeur of his mission, though his horizon was somewhat limited to the things of earth?

We must take the *whole* of a career before we pronounce upon it. We must not select a part here or a part there. Scripture stamps its broad clear character upon the personages that are its subjects. It sums up their life as on the whole of this or that complexion. Of one it says, "He wrought evil in the eyes of the Lord;" of another, "He did that which was right in the sight of the Lord." It shows how the timid Jacob had yet something in him which could develop into the saintlike, and be accepted before the seeming frank and genial Esau. It discerns in the rugged heroes of the Book of Judges an undercurrent of goodness, half-hidden beneath the turbid stream of their adventures, and a redeeming element of trust in God lurking in each one of them. It speaks of David in one place, in spite of the serious blots that marred that strong but tender spirit, as "the man after God's own heart." And what is the verdict of the sacred record on Hezekiah? " He did that which was right in the sight of the Lord," said (remember) of three Kings only of Judah. " He trusted in the Lord God of Israel, so that after him was none like him among all the Kings of Judah nor any that were before him." In the Apocrypha, he is classed among the three perfect rulers: "Except David, Hezekiah, and Josiah, all committed trespass."[1] Many would think they had reached the highest attainable ideal, did they deserve such a glowing eulogy. But for our instruction neither are his faults ignored.

Let us glance rapidly at his reign. From his father Ahaz—that weak and idolatrous ruler—he had inherited an empire much impaired in resources, and sadly demoralized in

---

[1] Ecclesiasticus, xlix. 4 (R. V.).

religion. He enters at once upon a course of reform, and by a happy conjuncture of circumstances, the best of kings is seconded by the noblest of prophets. The temple is cleansed. The brazen serpent, the time-honoured relic of the desert-wanderings, is destroyed, because abused by superstition. The passover is celebrated with a splendour unknown since the reign of Solomon. A new life dawned upon Judah. Nor can we forget his efforts in restoring the musical services of the temple; the revival of lyric poetry, after languishing for two centuries; the collection of many psalms that otherwise would have perished, and the addition of new ones. The era, too, of Hezekiah is the special era of prophecy, and the period of its highest development.

These are some of the brightest features of his reign. We must pass lightly over the great event of Sennacherib's invasion; his demands for tribute, at first rejected but afterwards complied with in humiliating terms. That striking chapter,[1] the siege, the peril, the deliverance, when

> "The Angel of Death spread his wings on the blast,
> And breathed on the face of the foe as he passed."

does it not live in the memory of all who have ever heard it read?

[1] 2 Kings, xix.

(2) We will come at once to the sickness of Hezekiah, our more immediate subject. The anxiety and the intense strain caused by the critical moment of its occurrence had no doubt brought it on, or in any case had aggravated it.

Those hours spent in the sick chamber at Jerusalem were no less monotonous, no less irksome and weary than are such hours now (what they are some of us can testify by experience). Could the feelings of an invalid be more faithfully described than they are in the plaintive language of the sick king when he says his tent was struck, his thread of life severed. "He will cut me off with pining sickness: from day even to night wilt thou make an end of me. . . . Like a crane or a swallow, so did I chatter: I did mourn as a dove. Mine eyes fail with looking upward: O Lord, I am oppressed: undertake for me."[1]
And next,—that intense desire for life, so noticeable in him—let us pause awhile to consider that. It was not in him, the shrinking, almost cowardly feeling that at first it might appear to be. This yearning for life varies much, we know, with circumstances, with health, with animal spirits. No doubt; in general, the truer instinct is that expressed by Tennyson :

[1] Isaiah, xxxviii. 12.

> "'Tis life whereof our nerves are scant,
> Oh, life, not death, for which we pant,
> More life and fuller that I want."

Times there are, that come to most of us, when, from no overweening pride of health, but rather, perhaps, from deepest gratitude, we feel this to the uttermost: times when it seems an insult to have the question put to us, "Is life worth living?" times when we can see nothing but its preciousness, its sacredness, its endless possibilities and opportunities for good. But should some startling calamity, or the sense of some insidious malady, jar upon our sense of security, should some cherished hope be crushed, some idol shattered, does not the desire for a better state lay hold of us with a new and more solemnizing power than we ever realized before? And even without this,—have we not seen the willingness to die (and that in no weak temper, no sad or sour spirit) exhibited by one or two of the noblest characters of our times? The late Prince Consort, shortly before his fatal illness, in speaking to the Queen, said, "I do not cling to life. I set no store by it. If I knew that those I love were well cared for, I should be quite ready to depart to-morrow." Did this arise from indifference or distaste for life? Far from it. None enjoyed it more keenly, none was happier or more cheerful in his work. But, like St. Paul, he was ready to be with Christ, which was far better, and death to him was but the portal to a higher sphere. And another whom no one ever accused of languor or stagnation felt something similar—I mean Charles Kingsley. To one who on his last American journey wished him long life he replied, "That is the last thing I desire. It may be, as we grow older, one acquires more and more the painful consciousness of the difference between what ought to be done and what can be done."

But to turn our thoughts back again over more than twenty-five centuries. In a monarch like Hezekiah, can we be surprised at expressions breathing something of a hopeless horror at the prospect of being deprived of the residue of his days? In that remote age some of the best of men trembled at dissolution as separating them from the light of the Divine presence. But most of all did they shrink from a premature end, as if it were a clear token of God's displeasure. "I said O my God, take me not away in the midst of my days." Added to this, in the case of Hezekiah, there were two strong feelings that we can hardly over-estimate. His life seemed essential for the promotion of God's glory. His energies seemed most needed after the shock so recently sustained by the nation. He was the mainstay of their confidence. And secondly, there was the desire to leave an heir to the throne, for as yet there was none. At the time of his death, fifteen years later, his son was only twelve, and therefore not yet born. Thus we see how patriotic and disinterested motives were blended with natural feelings in his prayer for restoration to life and prolongation of life.

(3.) That restoration was immediately granted; and on it, before concluding, I will ask you to dwell.

How will it now fare with the King? How will he stand the test? How will he play his part? We look with intense interest to the record of those added fifteen years. For here we have not indeed a Lazarus actually brought back from the sepulchre, but what is next to it, we have one rescued from the very gates of death. We can compare the state of suspense and dejection with the realized deliverance. Will those sick-bed vows prove fleeting and evanescent, "like showers across an April sky?" Or will the whole sequel of his life be purified, after it has passed through that crucible of suffering? We are not told much, but we can trace somewhat of its effects. We notice the tender, thankful spirit that breathes through the touching hymn written when peace had succeeded to anguish, and security to fear. "The living, the living he shall praise thee as I do this day: the father to the children shall make known thy truth." He reigns in honour and prosperity. He improves the capital in many ways. The shock given to Assyria had magnified Judah in the eyes of other nations, and distant princes send ambassadors to congratulate him on his recovery. Among them are some from Babylon. And here comes a weakness, a declension, a failure. Oh! how it must have grieved and disappointed his counsellor Isaiah, who sees at once through their flattery! With too much self-confidence, alas! and complacency he displays to them his accumulated treasures. He was not quite proof against this particular peril incident to the granting of his prayer.

And then, again, was the gift of a son, to sit upon his throne, an unmixed boon? For what manner of son did that heir prove himself to be? That heir was Manasseh, the very worst of all the kings, one from whose reign posterity turned away its eyes, or looked back on it as the lowest point of degradation. True, Hezekiah was spared the misery of witnessing the destruction of the fair edifice he had built up with such loving care, *felix opportunitate mortis*. But though when he died his son was but twelve, by the age of twelve, the character has begun to show itself, and some misgivings and forebodings of what was to come must have more than once dawned upon and disturbed the father.

And how will it fare with us, dear friends? *That* is the vital question, is it not, for each of us, should length of days (as may *not* be the case) be added to us? If tranquil happy times are ours, with scarce a cloud to ruffle their serenity—no anxiety about those we love, no shadow of doubt or distrust of their affection, no serious derangement of health—will our hearts be lifted up, as we see by his momentary lapse, that the heart of the King of Judah was lifted up? Shall we not rather be humbled, shall we not ascribe it all to God as its source, and pray Him to bless it all to us? Or if some sharp trial be sent, will we take it with us, as Hezekiah took the bitter, taunting letter of the Assyrian, into the house of the Lord, and spread it there before the Lord? Will you trust Him with your *whole* life, and leave the issues of it to Him? trust Him not merely at stated seasons of prayer, whether in private or here in this chapel, but trust Him with *all* your days. Yes, trust Him alike with your times of work and with your bright hours of recreation. Will you pray Him to defend you under His wings from dangers special to your Eton life—yes, special to this portion of it, the long, glorious summer days, to which you are naturally looking forward—from the pestilence of evil habits and evil thoughts that walketh in the darkness, and also from the vapid, frivolous, sauntering indolence that destroyeth in the noonday? Pause and reflect before your characters have crystallized, as in very much less than fifteen years they must crystallize, so that no great change in them will then be any longer possible: and when next tempted and tried where your armour is weakest (and we know each of us where that is), think, oh! think, I beg you, what it would be to hear said of you, not that you had not fifteen years or even months or weeks left you, but that you had not fifteen minutes, or may be twice fifteen minutes, before rendering your account.

> "Hamlet, thou art slain;
> No medicine in the world can do thee good,
> In thee there is not half an hour's life."

And this (unless we are cut off in a moment), yes, this or its equivalent we must hear. If we do not hear it from others, it will flash upon our inner consciousness, with the certainty of absolute conviction.

Warnings we have had too, have we not? on which I need not dwell, coming very near our homes. One has been taken from us.

The Recovery of Hezekiah.

After many weeks of painful illness borne with great patience; after many prayers offered up for him here,—"God's finger touched him and he slept." While you were in the enjoyment of your homes, He took him to his last and best home. One has been taken, and how many others have been left! In each case we must believe it was done in mercy. Oh, may these warnings not be lost upon any of us! In that supreme moment which has come to him, and must come to us, unless we have indeed built upon the Rock, what will it be to feel the world and all here slipping from beneath us?

> "O could we see that hour go by
>   Whilst youthful pulses stir,
> With all our future to forgive,
> We scarce could bear the sight, and live!
> —Thou who for us hast suffer'd death,
>   Remember we are men;
> Thou on the right hand of the throne,
>   Have mercy on us then!"[1]

And oh, lastly, let us use the interval, as if we felt it were (as in truth it is), but a very brief one. Let each holy season impart to us its special strength! Let us press onwards to-day. It is Rogation Sunday, the day of asking! to-day, when we are beckoned on to celebrate the Feast of Thursday next,—"to ascend

---

[1] Hymns by F. T. Palgrave.

in heart and mind to Christ, and with Him continually to dwell." Let us ask of Christ, and most assuredly He will grant us here and hereafter, the true, the higher, the better life; the life that brings forth not thorns and thistles, parents' tears and wasted opportunities, but such fruit as shall remain. He will grant us not the mere fifteen years it may be of prolonged and necessarily chequered existence, but an immortality of joy and glory,—" the haven where we would be" won at last: the "house not builded with hands, eternal in the heavens." So may that word come true of each one of us, " He asked life of thee, and thou gavest him a long life, even for ever and ever."

Sermon XII.

A FAREWELL.[1]

"Peter seeing him saith to Jesus, Lord, and what shall this man do?"—*St. John*, xxi. 21.

THE chapter in which these words have been preserved is one of the most precious of the Divine records. When we read a passage like this, standing by itself, so full of interest, so rich in details, so solemn and unearthly in its whole tone and character, we are led to prize more highly than perhaps we have ever yet done, every page and every incident, every gracious look or word or act of our Lord, treasured up for us by one or other of the Evangelists.

Above all we are led, in this instance, to reflect how great were our loss, were this fourth Gospel removed from our Bibles; so intimately bound up as it is with the very heart and core of the creed of Christendom,—the battlefield, as it has been truly called, of the New Testament; the record in which are enshrined side

[1] July 8th, 1883.

by side the tenderest companionship with Jesus, and the strongest witness to His Divinity; the rock against which the surging waves of scepticism have persistently beaten, but evermore have beaten in vain.

In this concluding chapter, added evidently at a later date, after the rest of the Gospel had been completed, the beloved disciple's recollections are enshrined of one of the last appearances of Christ before His Ascension: principally, no doubt, to dispel the error growing up about himself that he should not die. But we can trace another object that the writer had in view. The second miraculous draught of fishes is narrated with such minuteness, as to point to a further purpose, and that is to be found in the whole of the conversation which grew out of the miracle.

We can touch but very rapidly upon the impressive scene, full of interest and full of instruction as it is.

The disciples had gone back to their own homes and their own occupations, in trustful waiting. They were again fishing in the blue waters of the Galilean lake, that lake that had been so eventful in the last three years of their lives. Through the night they had caught nothing. But as the day was breaking, there stood on the shelving beach One whom they failed to recognize, calling to them, "Children, have ye aught to eat?" And then, on His bidding them cast the net on the right side of the ship, the truth flashes instinctively on St. John, *It is the Lord*. Full of great fishes the net is drawn unbroken to the land, where they find the morning meal already spread, and the Lord, "Himself their host, waiting to give rather than to receive."[1] It was after that solemn, mysterious meal, a symbol doubtless of the Great Festival to be held upon the everlasting shore of Heaven,— that the searching question was put to Peter, "Lovest thou Me?" Thrice is it put, and in answer to the reiterated assurance of personal attachment ($\varphi\iota\lambda\tilde{\omega}\ \sigma\epsilon$) the threefold Apostolic charge is given, and the issues of that personal love are revealed;—the decline of the old impetuous vigour;—the feeble arms stretched out on the Cross—the death by which he should glorify God. And then the final command that could turn weakness into strength and the pangs of martyrdom into the joy of self-surrender, *Follow thou Me*.

They were walking along the side of the lake: and we may suppose that St. Peter with our Lord was slightly in front of the rest, when he turns and sees his favourite friend and chosen companion following behind

---

[1] Westcott, "The Revelation of the Risen Lord," vi.

them, as though silently signifying that he too was ready to follow whithersoever his Master might lead him. The question, prompted by loving interest in the fortunes of his brother-apostle naturally rises to his lips, *Lord, and what shall this man do?* In the original it is still more brief and rapid, *Lord, and this man what?* What of him? what shall he do or suffer? What glimpse of *his* destiny, what indication of the path before *him* wilt Thou reveal? The man of active energy would fain know something of the man of contemplation. So may one here show a wistful anxiety about a comrade, whose pursuits and tastes are very different from his own. So may the young man, before whom a busy public life lies already marked out, ask with affectionate wonder what career is in store for his school-fellow of more retiring habits and less ambitious temperament? The more buoyant, self-confident, eager character, is not indifferent to the fortunes of his more quiet neighbour. The humble may inquire about those whom it feels to be far better than itself. There was genuine, sincere interest in St. Peter's question: but there was also some tinge of curiosity, some desire perhaps to know and to guide another's life and work at the risk of weakening the force of his own. Our Saviour's answer seems to check this spirit so far as it required checking: "If I will that he tarry till I come, what is that to thee? follow thou Me." It is characteristic of the way in which He constantly met His questioners. It is so characteristic of it that, if proof were needed (which it is not) of the genuineness of this last chapter, it might be found in this reply of Christ. You remember the solemn answer with which He met the spirit of unwise, though not unnatural curiosity shewn in asking, "Lord, are there few that be saved?" "Strive," He said, "strive to enter in at the strait gate," turning the thoughts of the questioner into a healthier and more profitable channel. The answer in this instance is partly special, dealing with the individual case before Him. "If I will that he abide while I come: if I will that he survive that great shaking of the earth and heaven in the destruction of the Holy City, what is that to thee? Go on thy way, straightforward, and cast no look behind." It is partly universal, for us and for all ages. *Follow thou Me.* Trust and wait.

Each phase and development of character, however diverse,—each life with all its manifold windings and perplexities, lies spread out as an open map before His unerring gaze. Leave to Him the fashioning, the ordering, the disposal of it all, whether for thyself or for thy friends. Do the work appointed thee, without haste and without pause, without anxiety and without self-confidence. To the end, whatever that end may be, through disappointments or through successes, through the tangled course of events (as they seem to you), however different the shape they assume from what you looked for—in glowing health or in the sick chamber, cheered and encouraged, sustained and invigorated by My Presence, *Follow thou Me.*

We pause not this morning to dwell upon the future of the Great Apostle, about whom St. Peter asked: the thirty years' silence and seclusion; the patient tarrying; the precious contributions at last added to seal and complete the sacred volume.

To-day, when the time for parting is drawing near for so many of those before me, the application of the text is so obvious, so urgent, and so inevitable that we must hasten to it at once. For we cannot but hear in it a warning voice, an alarum to rouse us to very serious and very practical reflections. Not assuredly that we would attempt to label any individual character, or prejudge any career: not that we would forecast the mysterious future of any son of Eton, whose time here is drawing to its close. But speaking broadly, and limiting ourselves to certain representative types, may we not pray and hope that some word may be spoken in season, that the arrow may in some cases fly to its mark, and press home the momentous question, What shall this man do?

What shall this youth do, who is standing upon the very verge and opening of manhood? the border-land of two stages of education, looking back on the education of this place, and looking forward to the education of the University? The education of school must (if he review it calmly and impartially—if he is honest with himself), must, I say, have revealed to him something of his real inner being. Can he help acknowledging in the retrospect some falling off from the higher standard he originally set before himself? Can he but feel some compunction, some regrets at having insufficiently grappled with the evil within him? Is he not at any rate conscious of some faulty tendencies to make him pause, to cause him apprehension and stir him to greater vigilance?

How is he prepared to go forth upon the wider arena, to use without abusing the less restricted liberty, to meet and to endure the unknown ordeal that is certain in one direction or another to shape and mould his maturer habits, upon more rigid and more indelible lines?

Oh! how much may hinge upon those next

three or four years! Will he take what should be the seed-plot of a life's usefulness, and treat it as a mere playground? I will not contemplate the prospect of one who wastes term and vacation on reckless expenditure, or on one who is led on gradually but surely through the flowery paths of dissipation, till he become the victim of those grosser temptations that assail our lower nature. He may indeed be saved, yet so as by fire; but he will bear through life the scars and wounds of such an encounter. God grant that he may never fall so low! God grant that he may never incur so tremendous a risk! Still let me say, in all earnestness, that it is *not* a mere matter of course that this may not happen when the current sets strongly in the direction given it by some tyrant passion. It is not of course that he keep the one true path, if he once relax his hold upon the vital safeguards of religion; upon *Prayer*, and *Vigilance*, and *Endurance*.

But granted that he rise superior to these graver perils. Will he, when he leaves these walls, fall into other snares? Will he palter with the priceless opportunities that are his? Will he fritter away his time on trifles? Will he allow himself to be drawn into the vortex of frivolity, and abuse the egitimate refreshments of social intercourse? Will he regard the amusements of boyhood as the adequate end and object of life? instead of feeling that they are fair and good and have their place and use, but that to put them ever first, is to invert the relative proportions of things? Will he emancipate himself from some unworthy traditions or some narrow code of fashion, that hitherto he may have cherished? Will he gain a larger view of life by converse with robuster minds—no longer echo the prejudices of others, but learn to judge for himself on the great questions of right and wrong? The choice of a profession will have dawned already upon some of you. But the choice of a definite line of study, out of the many that offer themselves, cannot safely be deferred. That *some* line of serious study must be selected may be assumed, for why else go at all to a place whose final cause is the building up of the fabric of the mind? Little do those who look with pity or with supercilious indifference upon the University student know what they are forfeiting. They are forfeiting, in most cases, the power of doing solid work in the world. It is not a mere question of extending the subjects of school studies; of acquiring a command over some portions of history; a grasp of and critical insight into the systems of ancient philosophy. The case is widely different from this. Apart from the bracing and disciplining of the mind, those to whom steady persevering adherence to some one line of study is a mystery and enigma, are losing what they would give anything hereafter to recover. *The capability of sustained toil is not a thing to be taken up when and how you choose.* It is not a matter depending on an effort of the will at any time or under any circumstances. It is the outcome and the fruit of training. It is a treasure; a treasure not casually lighted upon by the indolent or the *dilettante;* but the result of searching and delving with a reasonable prospect of discovery. And when this power of work takes the form of labour for others, what fairer sight can we see, what securer basis is there for the love and admiration of your fellow-men? Who are those who most earn the gratitude of their age? where is the likeness of the lineaments of Christ most to be traced? Is it not in such as will bend themselves to severe work; who have prepared themselves to discover and to choose the best causes to which to devote their energies? and this power of service, this noble zeal to "scorn delights and live laborious days," depend upon it, will be more and more in request from all classes (high as well as low) amidst the accumulating problems of the times in which you will have to live.

Lord, and what shall this man do? this one, who has mastered passion, or at least will not be her slave? who has the genuine thirst for knowledge, who is fired with the zeal for true enlightenment of mind? In this higher and purer region is there still no danger? Yes, much, though of a different kind. There is pride of intellect, there is intense and undue absorption in the task of self-culture to be guarded against. Will such a one shut himself up in the past and be blind to the momentous interests and lessons of the present? Will he stand aloof from his fellows in fancied self-improvement, and lose the varied play of mind, the interchange of thought which constitutes half the value of College life? And then as maturer age draws on, will he take no part in the sounding labour-house of life, but look on at it from outside —finding fault with this or that part of the machinery with fastidious smile—criticising everything, himself constructing nothing? Or again, will he give the rein to free inquiry? Shall he become deeply versed in German metaphysics or French criticism, while the grand old Hebrew record and Christ's words of eternal life pall upon him and are slighted or forgotten? Oh! let him return to them day by day! Let him be sure that he will need them more than ever now, to sober and to humble him, to save him at the last from that saddest utterance of the Roman Emperor[1]—strenuous and unwearied as was his energy and industry—*Omnia fui et nihil expedit.*

Lord, and what shall this man do? This one who has learnt to conquer self in these its more insidious and subtle forms? Who will regard his physical strength but as a trust committed to him, and his body but as the ready instrument of his soul? Who will bring the gold of his philosophy and solid learning, and the myrrh of his poetry and lighter accomplishments, and the frankincense of all those gentler graces and courtesies that shed a charm round the worker, and prevent him from seeming hard and cold and repellent, and will lay them all at the feet of his Master.

Rather shall we not say, "what will such a one *not* do?" Whether his character be cast in the mould of the ardent energetic Peter, or of the thoughtful, patient, contemplative John?

I have spoken but of one branch of after-life to those who are about to leave; but in truth the spirit of hearty work on which we have dwelt is the same for all its phases. What

---

[1] Septimius Severus.

shall this and this man do in the various paths to which he may be summoned?

What shall he *do*, we say? Yes, but recollect that to do in the sense of to achieve something brilliant, is granted only to the gifted few. It is not necessary for us to do anything heroic, it *is* necessary for us to strive to be perfect. "Perfection is being, not doing. In Christian life, every moment and every act is an opportunity for doing the one thing of becoming Christ-like."[1] Still let me press on all, two great principles of action: First, the duty of aiming at personal influence, "the key of great movements," as it has been called, "the soul of all that is deep and powerful, both in what lasts and in what makes change."[2] And how far you will exert personal influence, depends very largely upon what you are here. Be pure, be courageous, be merciful, be unswerving in right-doing now, and you will be centres of good; you will radiate light on all around you hereafter.

And secondly, have enthusiasm: enthusiasm for some noble cause, which by the antagonistic power of good shall cast out and leave no place for the mean, the trivial, the

---

[1] F. W. Robertson, "Christian Progress by Oblivion of the Past."

[2] Dean Church, University Sermons.

ignoble: enthusiasm, the handmaid of the Faith that removes mountains, and of the Love that thinks the best it can of all; the antidote of sloth, and of depression: Enthusiasm, which (be it said with reverence) was in Christ, when He was consumed with a holy zeal for His Father's House, and when He rejoiced or exulted in spirit, on beholding Satan as lightning fall from heaven. Have enthusiasm for your school, for your country, for your own future! Who would not choose the enthusiastic with all his liability to error, rather than the cold marble character of one who walks too cautiously ever to stumble; but narrows his horizon to the things of earth, and never lifts his gaze to heaven?

And yet one word more, which not to utter would be affectation in him who addresses you. Were he not to express the sense of what he owes to this place, "the stone would" indeed "cry out of the wall, and the beam out of the timber would answer it," to reprove him. Bear with him if he does so for a few moments. As his life here passes silently before him: profoundly conscious as he is of many failings and shortcomings as boy and as master: from that day distant but never to be forgotten. when he was brought here, and committed like you by a mother's tender prayer and aspirations, to the perils of a public school,—here where every footstep calls up associations of some old companionship, some kind, cheering word, some germ it may be of thought and resolve,—this Eton which must remain till death blended indissolubly with all that is most sacred and precious to him—what should be the predominant feeling on going from it to a sphere where watchfulness and prayer and patience will be needed more than ever? Surely it should be humbled thoughts and thankfulness. "Tho' much is taken, much abides." If there are memories of sharpest sorrow, there are memories also of undeserved blessings. When a few Sundays since I listened to my valued friend and colleague (once with me in the same pupil-room, and for many years united with me in our common work here) preaching from this pulpit; when a fortnight ago, I heard an honoured pupil addressing the rest of our body in their Chapel; when we can trace (what is far better than their triumphs) the steady growth in goodness of those we have taught; or when one sees reflected in pupils the features of their fathers who were with us here, and recognize in them the same generous spirit,—the thought must arise, that this continuity of affection, this handing on of the lamp of truth and knowledge, this perpetual self-renewal of youth amidst the old scenes, are among the things that add a zest to existence, far beyond its vaunted prizes.

> "This does not come with houses or with gold,
> 'Tis not in the world's market bought and sold."

Oh, let us treasure to the utmost such a heritage! "Thanks to the human heart by which we live." Let it not be for nothing that we have been brought up under the shadow of a venerable past! At least let us give this proof of sincerity and loyalty, that we perform the duties of these few remaining weeks conscientiously, punctually, and unflinchingly. Let us gather up the fragments that remain of a school-time, of a boyhood, of a life! Whatever be the future in store for you, lofty or humble, arduous or tranquil, whether it be to battle for the rights of man in the great Council-Chamber of the nation, to rule some vast and distant province, or to minister for Christ in some lowly hamlet, remember that "*to whom much has been given, of the same shall much be required.*"

Continue in the things that you have learnt in the sweet services of this Chapel. Follow Christ, in an ordered sober life of self-control, which is only another term for His easy yoke. Strive to do nothing unworthy of your Alma Mater. Strive to promote her true welfare!

For her and for all her sons the fervent prayer shall go up:

> "Peace be within thy walls,
>   And plenteousness within thy palaces.
> For my brethren and companions' sakes,
>   I will wish thee prosperity.
> Yea, because of the house of the Lord our God,
>   I will seek to do thee good."

Sermon XIII.

THE HEALING OF THE DEMONIAC BOY.[1]

"But Jesus rebuked the unclean spirit, and healed the boy, and gave him back to his father."—*St. Luke*, ix. 42 (R. V.).

CAN we not almost see that agonized father going down on his knees to Christ? Can we not hear his passionate entreaty, "Lord, have mercy on my son, for he is epileptic, and suffereth grievously. I beseech Thee to look upon him, for he is mine only child, and behold a spirit taketh him, and he suddenly crieth out, and it teareth him that he foameth, and it hardly departeth from him, bruising him sorely. Ofttimes it hath cast him into the fire and into the water to destroy him. And I besought thy disciples to cast him out, and they could not."

And then, that graphic account in St. Mark, giving all the unmistakable symptoms of the malady, and how our Lord, pierced to the heart by the distressful scene that burst upon

[1] June 19th, 1892.

Him—the inquisitive crowd, the wrangling scribes, the failure of the disciples trusting to exorcise the demon by the mere magic of His Name, said, "*Bring him unto Me;*" how no sooner did the poor stricken boy meet Jesus' eye than he was seized by a fresh paroxysm, the worst of all Christ had ever confronted; how He questioned the half-despairing father, as a kind physician would do, and drew out his faltering faith and accepted it, weak as it was in its expression, "*Lord, I believe, help thou mine unbelief.*" How at last Jesus spake the word of irresistible power, and then—though not till after another and yet direr seizure—a spasm that convulsed the whole frame, and left him rigid and still as a corpse, the demon departed from him. Then Jesus took him gently by the hand, and raised him up calm and tranquillized after that desolating storm, and gave him back to his father, *and the boy was healed from that hour.*

It is a scene in the gospel history most vividly brought before us by all the three first Evangelists.

Is it only that? Does it only deal with a condition of things long since passed away, a set of phenomena peculiar to the time and place when and where Christ's life was spent upon earth? Has it no counterpart in our own age? Has it no special lesson for us here this morning—yes, for you whom I especially address?

Surely it bears with it this most comforting truth, that the temptations, the trials that beset boyhood, whatever they be, and wherever they are permitted for a time to overcloud the sunshine of youth, whether as then under Syrian skies, or in English homes, or amidst the flower and hope of England's coming race, are indeed sympathized with by Christ, and that the thraldom of the Evil Spirit, that so vexes and possesses, can be overmastered and conquered by Christ, and by Him alone.

"*And Jesus rebuked the devil, and he departed from him, and the boy was healed from that hour.*"

I detached part of one verse, as my text, and yet one feels that it can hardly be dissociated from the whole of the foregoing narrative. It is closely connected with the subject of the Transfiguration, as that centra event in Christ's ministry had itself a twofold aspect; on the one side being a glimpse of the final glory, and on the other being linked to His decease, the subject you remember of the discourse on the Mount, the ignominious details of that decease being for the first time deliberately and distinctly announced to the startled three on their way down immediately afterwards. So, too, with this sad story. It has another side to it. The most opposite things are brought together. They are so connected we know on the canvas of Raphael. Up above is the radiance that emanates from the very fountain of light; down below, poor humanity with its struggles, its passions, its vain attempts to cope with misery, its wrangling, its failure. Agitation, alarm, helplessness, malicious pleasure at the discomfiture of the disciples are depicted on the different countenances, while the open volume seems to suggest the idea of some spell or form of words having been tried, as if perchance it might succeed. Up above, all is perfect peace, serene tranquillity; down below, all is strife, trouble, and unrest.

It is true that the two events could not really have synchronized; for the vision took place at night, and St. Luke tells us that it was on the following day that our Lord was met by the crowd. Still there is, is there not, a deep truth underlying that picture, the last that Raphael ever painted, the one which after his death was hung with its lower part unfinished, over his bier, in the chamber where he was accustomed to work?

There are occasions like the present when the sweet and solemn services of this chapel, revisited for the first time on a Sunday after an interval of several years, touch the feelings and raise the spirit in an unwonted manner. And to many of you I can well believe that times of refreshing come each week, and at each service in the week that you attend here. But we have each of us to go back again to our duties—homely, and even irksome as they may be—in our several spheres in this work-a-day world.

St. Peter, while on the Mount, in the presence of those two glorified saints (whose luminous bodies were a prophetic intimation of the brightness of the redeemed in their after form), was carried beyond himself in an ecstasy of delight, rapt into another world in the bliss of that heavenly communion. While gazing on his transfigured Master he felt strong in the spirit, and wished to remain where he was. "It is good for us to be here." But he could not remain there. He had to go back again and to face all the suffering that awaited them at the foot of the Mount. He had to hear very soon of such coming shame and agony as he had never imagined possible. And we, too, must rely upon no mere momentary fervour, no transient emotion. The conflict with evil has to be renewed again and again. After a nearer insight into heaven it is often sharper than before. After coming to the Holy Communion it is more necessary

Healing of the Demoniac Boy.

than ever to be watchful. Indeed, as Bishop Ken says, "it is then that your greatest work is but beginning."

I know not whether there are any specially new forms of evil of which I should speak, or whether there exist foes more to be dreaded by you now than there used to be in this place; but I know from my own experience and memory of school how hard the Tempter tries to ruin, and I know also, from a later and much more lengthened experience, how he is ever sowing tares among the wheat, and doing all he can to mar the good work going on in this favoured place, where, with so many advantages, with such helps and blessings as it possesses, it ought not to be so difficult to be good. It is not to be believed that he has relaxed the virulence of his hatred, or the pertinacity of his assaults, or that he will ever do so, so long as evil exists.

Is it using too strong language to say that he has ofttimes ere now cast many a youth of fairest promise *into the fire and into the water, to destroy him?* into the fire of some strong over-mastering passion—some uncurbed desire, some fatal habit—and that, too, in spite of the tenderest memories and claims of home, and of grave remonstrance, and affectionate warning of tutors?

Is it too much to say, after that—when the

horror of such a falling away comes home to the young and as yet unseared conscience—when the glory and the loveliness of the life once known is seen to be departed—when the thought arises, "*where shall I hide my forehead and my eyes?*" "Can I ever be like that again?" "Can I ever know the simplicity, the joy of that comparative innocence?"—when companions of stronger will drag down—whispering, "it is no good, what is the use of trying to be better than everyone else?"—when the misdeeds of the past seem to throw their baleful shadow over the whole coming future,—is it too much to say that the Evil One casts the poor lad into the waters—the deep waters of despair—for a time, or else into the stagnant, fetid, deadly waters of indifference, and coldness, and apathy to all higher impulse? But even out of that hottest furnace, even out of those deadly waters, there is an escape:

> "At last I heard a voice upon the slope,
> Cry to the summit, Is there any Hope?"

Yes, the Healer is already on the way. He is coming down from the Mount. He is leaving all its glories to come to you. He is entering into and sympathizing with all the difficulties and fierce trials of boyhood. He is hastening to help you. He is very near. In a few moments He will be standing by you and rebuking the evil spirit that has such a hold over you, whatever it be, however pertinacious and inveterate!

"*And he gave the boy back to his father.*" Let us not miss that touching conclusion given us by St. Luke. Yes! He will give you back to reverence for yourself, to confiding thoughts, to the deeper love of your earthly parent, and of your Heavenly Father, both of which for a time you fancied you had forfeited for ever. He will never refuse His aid so long as the Prayer of Faith, "Lord, I believe, help Thou mine unbelief," be sincerely lifted up to him. He will command the demon to depart; He will so powerfully and so thoroughly expel it, that it shall not merely go out of itself, to return after a season with seven others more evil than itself, but He will cast it out. Oh! if I could make the echo of that vital distinction—as I first heard it long ago from Bishop Wilberforce—ring in your ears again! for is not this indeed the lesson of that poor possessed boy, that we never rest till the voice of sovereign power and authority go forth? Till not merely one bad habit give place to another, as the fiery passions and impetuosities of early life are so often followed by the colder calculating vices of age,—avarice, moroseness, hardness,—but the whole man is renovated, and the purified nature is made fit to be a temple for the Holy Spirit, instead of the resort of everything that can defile and disturb.

These that I have touched on are the more serious, the fiercer, the more terrible assaults on the citadel of Christian boyhood. There are others of a different kind, subtle and insidious rather than violent,—infirmities of character, lowerings of the tone and influence of your lives,—which still cannot be set right by any mere efforts of your own, but call for the hand of the Divine Healer.

There is the cynical or the critical spirit of one who is content to look on at the efforts toward higher good,—the storm and stress and struggle going on outside itself,—giving no help, but steering clear of it as far as may be. I do but glance at this. There is another danger, almost the opposite one, on which I would say a little ; it may not apply to many, but it may come home to some. I mean the restless, feverish desire to make a name, to win applause, the intolerance of all that looks like mediocrity or failure, the haunting idea, the suggestion implied or hinted that if you cannot excel in one line you must in another, that school life is a very poor thing unless you are to the front and make a decided mark in some branch or other of its pursuits and interests. This is indeed the abuse of a noble thing, the excess of a right feeling, and therefore one would not willingly be misunderstood in speaking of it, for who would breathe a syllable against lofty ambition and enthusiasm? There is far too little of it here or elsewhere; still I venture to think that secret pain and trouble is sometimes caused by such reflection on those who are not fitted, or not as yet fitted for the keener struggles and severer competitions. But why should they go out of their proper nature to strive after that for which they are not suited?

The great Head Master, Dr. Arnold (the fiftieth anniversary of whose death was commemorated last Sunday) once said, "If there be one thing on earth which is truly admirable, it is to see God's wisdom blessing an inferiority of natural powers where they have been honestly, truly, and zealously cultivated." Let them lay to heart those words. Let them not be discouraged. Let them not mind if they do not reach fame here. Early distinction is indeed often the herald of later eminence; but it is not always so, or of necessity so. Some of the men in the very first rank at the present day, whose words are listened to with the greatest respect, won no special honour, while at Eton, whether as scholars or as athletes. They went quietly along their way. They had a reserve of strength, due in part to daily tasks unostentatiously performed, and in their case it has come true that

> "Not once or twice in our fair island-story
> The path of duty was the way to glory."

If the rather exaggerated deference shown to the successful and the popular be sometimes a little trial to temper, if the pride of strength seem at times to trample down the less robust nature, let the thought come back of the serene, peace-breathing presence of Christ, calming all that jarring discord and unseemly strife for triumph at the foot of the mount. By taking His easy yoke you will find rest to your souls, and will win the true honour that comes from above, and is sure to come eventually to those who deserve it. Other distinctions you will let come and go as He shall bid them.

And so we are brought back again to the truth interpreted in the great picture. The peace of Heaven lies very near (if we seek for it) to all the wrangling and tumults, the weakness and helplessness of earth. The radiance of the Transfiguration is shining down upon the disconsolate father and upon his stricken boy. When Christ comes, He brings with Him bright glimpses of glory still lingering around Him. The force, the energy required

to vanquish the stubborn evil spirit, whateve
it be, however malignant, and however inveterate, is indeed great, superhuman. But it
is there. It is ready to be put forth. Everything depends upon faith, in the want oɩ
which lay the secret of failure hitherto. "*If
thou canst!* all things are possible to him that
believeth."

The Lord's arm is not shortened that it
cannot save. To Him we must turn. By
none else can the deliverance be wrought out.

"Oh tortuous paths!" says St. Augustine,
"woe to the presumptuous spirit that hopes,
if it withdraws from Thee, that it will find
anything better. Thou alone art our Rest.
Thou alone settest us free from our miserable
wanderings, and establishest our goings in
Thy way."[1]

[1] "Confessions," bk. vi., ch. xvi.

Sermon XIV.

GOD'S LAMP NEVER EXTIN-GUISHED.[1]

"The lamp of God was not yet gone out."—1 *Samuel*, iii. 3 (R. V.).

VERY beautiful is the sight of unsullied youth ministering in holy places, separate from contact with the outer world, wholly devoted to religious service. Even in the cult of a heathen god, when we meet with anything resembling such a dedication of the freshest period of life, we cannot help being arrested by its charm. The young Ion[2] in Greek Tragedy has a strange fascination for us, as he tends the altar of Apollo at Delphi, as he scares away the birds that swoop down from the cliffs of Parnassus; as he sings his joyous

---

[1] June 18th, 1893.

[2] κλεινὸς δ' ὁ πόνος μοι,
θεοῖσιν δούλαν χέρ' ἔχειν,
οὐ θνατοῖς, ἀλλ' ἀθανάτοις . . .
εἴθ' οὕτως ἀεὶ Φοίβῳ
λατρεύων μὴ παυσαίμαν, ἢ
παυσαίμαν ἀγαθᾷ μοίρᾳ.
        EURIP. *Ion*, 130.

morning hymn, boasting that his ministrations are rendered to no mortal, but to the immortals, and praying that such happy toil as his may never cease, but with his life. How much more lovely is the vision of the son of many prayers, the child-priest, Samuel, girded with his linen ephod, consecrated from the first to the true God in the tabernacle at Shiloh! The historian seems gladly to pause in his narrative of those dark days that were calling down swift destruction upon priest and people, in order to linger awhile over the picture of the blameless lad of twelve years old, tending the Sanctuary by day, lying down within its precincts by night, and opening its doors at sunrise. Other pictures of childhood and youth spent in special service to God we have brought before us in Scripture. We have one of Josiah, who in the eighth year of his reign (*i.e.*, when he was but sixteen years old) took the first steps in that reform which he afterwards carried out so fully. Of him the record is that "*while he was yet young, he began to seek after the God of David his father.*" We have another in Timothy, of whose early days St. Paul gives us a glimpse: "*From a child* thou hast known the Holy Scriptures, which are able to make thee wise unto salvation, through faith which is in Christ Jesus." But far, far beyond all, we have Him—before whom all images of early innocence and guilelessness grow faint and pale—the Holy Child, who, when he was twelve years old was found in His Father's house, bent on doing His Father's business, sitting in the Temple, in the midst of the astonished doctors of the law, both hearing and asking them questions. Well might such an ideal of unearthly devotedness inspire (as in most of the instances mentioned, it has inspired) the pencil of artists!

The scene in the sanctuary at Shiloh—the deep silence of the early morning—the young child hearing a voice and mistaking it at first in a childish manner; the contrast between him and the aged Eli, feeble and infirm of will, having to hear his doom from the lips of his own pupil who was to succeed him as Judge—there is no need to dwell on it. It is a scene which once read fixes itself indelibly upon the memory.

Let us return to the text: "*The lamp of God was not yet gone out,*" as we read it in the Revised Version, for "ere the lamp of God went out." There were times—many times—in the history of Israel when that lamp was all but extinguished. There was the period when the hideous worship of the Phœnicians had been imported by Ahab to rival the worship of Jehovah, the moment when it seemed even to Elijah that all was lost; yet even then amidst the growing apostasy, the Lord had kept to Himself those 7,000 who were secretly faithful, and had not bowed the knee to Baal. There was the time of deepest degradation into which the nation sunk when transplanted to Babylon, but even then the voice of the prophets of the Captivity was heard, and Judah was to rise from her ashes, and a new era was to dawn. And so it has been again and again; there have been periods of gloom when it might seem that the lamp was to go out; but at such critical moments the sacred fire has ever been burning, there have been "the few names even in Sardis which have not defiled their garments,"—the ten righteous men—the custodians of the dying flame—the regenerators and survivors of Christ's Church.

In the final horrors of the Siege of Rome by Alaric, the lamp of God was not extinguished. It burnt on with undying light, and some striking examples of Christian goodness and mercy relieved the general gloom. The belief in the divinity of Rome, so long and so passionately clung to by the heathen, could not survive the fall of her temples and idols; but was it not just then, when the discredited city seemed crumbling into ruin, that St. Augustine put forth his great work, "The City of God"? appealing in it to conscience,

O

appealing to past history, and justifying the ways of Providence to man? And the more that research is carried into any parts of what we call the Dark Ages, not yet fully explored, probably the more will the words of our text be illustrated. At the close of the sixth century, Ireland was the centre of light and learning, and from Ireland there radiated beams of missionary enterprise to the north and to the east: we see Columba bearing the lamp to Iona, and a little later on Columban penetrating the wild forests of the Vosges. The worst miseries, perhaps, that Europe ever has known, were witnessed during the eighth, ninth, and tenth centuries. Yet even in those desert tracts here and there an oasis appears.

Karl,—the great Charles[1]—stands out, as has been finely said, "like a beacon upon a waste, or a rock in the broad ocean." Stained as he was with some vices, he must still be regarded as wonderfully enlightened when contrasted with the barbarian world around him. And then look at our noble-hearted Alfred! What historical character so nearly approaches perfection? Weak in body, and "at the head of a weak and degenerate society whose hour of dissolution had wellnigh struck,"[2] how gal-

[1] Hallam, "Middle Ages," ch. i., pt. i.
[2] Merivale, "The Romans under the Empire," ch. lxviii., in his comparison of M. Aurelius with Alfred.

lantly he struggled on! Surely he is the very type of the Happy Warrior,

> "The generous Spirit, who, when brought
> Among the tasks of real life, hath wrought
> Upon the plan that pleased his boyish thought:
> Whose high endeavours are an inward light
> That makes the path before him always bright."

The Lamp of God was not yet gone out in England under such a ruler; no, nor when those drearier and desperate times ensued, when in the expressive figure of the Church Historian [1] "Christ seemed to be asleep in the hinder part of the vessel." The benefits conferred upon mediæval life by the Monasteries cannot be ignored; the greatest of them were founded before the Conquest, and in them were nurtured some men who in self-denial, in singleness of purpose and courage, have seldom been surpassed.

The close of the tenth century was the close of an iron age. "Men's hearts everywhere were failing them for fear and for looking after those things which were coming upon the earth." But no sooner was the dreaded one thousandth year passed, than the skies seemed to become serener, and Hope renewed itself. The Christian world received a new impulse

---

[1] Cardinal Baronius.

and from the religious excitement of that date, and out of its agonies and birth-pangs, arose the dawn of Christian Art in Europe. The lamp of Norman architecture was lit, if not to inspire the beauty and devotion of its successor, yet still breathing awe and solemnity in its massive creations. Thus we see that

> "Sprinkled along the waste of years
> Full many a soft green isle appears."

There was the lamp of *missionary zeal* in the sixth and seventh, there was the lamp of *architecture* beginning to illuminate even the last years of the tenth century, and destined to burst forth into a magnificent future.

There is a *third lamp*, which was to shine forth with more and more brilliance after the revival of letters, but which even before that had sent forth no obscure rays—I mean the lamp of *education*. Time forbids my dwelling on it: but here, if anywhere, in this training ground of character, and within the walls of this chapel, with its hallowed associations and far-reaching memories, it could not be passed by in silence. Light out of darkness, hope out of despair, order out of disorder,—is not that the teaching of the mediæval times, and, we may trust, of all history? It was a time of national discontent, distress, and disorganization when Wiclif died, but he was a morning star, heralding the coming daylight. And nine years after Wiclif's death, just five hundred years ago, when William of Wykeham founded Winchester, and about the time whence several Colleges at both Universities date their charters —the lamp of God assuredly had not gone out in England. It was a period, too, saddened by defeat abroad, and troubled by factions at home, a period of the utmost depression in literature and learning, when not quite half a century later the good work of Henry VI. was begun, and the first stone was laid of the chapel in which we worship God to-day. And not less from the annals of our church and our nation in their sequel might the truth of our text be illustrated. The religious condition of England during the last century will occur to every one as an instance. "There have been seasons of torpor and depression, but after each such interval Christ's Church has manifested her own recuperative power."

Perhaps I may seem already to have dwelt too long upon the past, although in but a fragmentary manner, in this glance across the pages of history, long before Eton was known as a place devoted to learning. But to any thoughtful mind must not the past have a perpetual value? We cannot, if we would, dissociate ourselves from it. And just as with nations their present rests on and is but the outcome of all their past, so it is with individuals. Our character is continually being constructed upon what is vanishing and out of sight. It is every day being built up upon the sinking, subsiding, yet still sustaining reefs of our past.

I forego to pause upon the long roll of Eton's illustrious sons. To dwell upon such a record is sometimes to run the risk of ministering to complacent pride rather than to rouse to an imitation of their virtues. And I will only say of these latter days of our school's history, that the lamp of God has assuredly not gone out in them with the rise and extension of such good work in East London as they have witnessed. In the few words that remain, I would desire to deepen in you the sense of the immense value of the lamp burning in each one of you, which is nothing less than God's Holy Spirit; how very serious must the danger be of putting out that light, given you to be your guide through life's journey; how necessary to guard against letting it gradually get low,—against the relaxing of vigilance; dropping morning or evening prayer for one day, and the next day finding it hard to take it up again; the coming to Holy Communion hurriedly or carelessly, or not coming at all;—the trusting to any false lights, like those lit by the cruel wrecker to lure the ship upon the rocks, instead of to the sure Word of God, which is "a lantern to your feet, and a light unto your paths." It is thus that the lamp begins to fail and flicker, till at last it goes out.

Hand on the torch to others! Not only have light in yourselves, but be centres of light, radiating it to others! Hand it on, and take care that you hand it on not less bright than you received it! Let your ideal of Eton be a noble, a worthy one! Whatever it may be given you to accomplish, let there be ever associated with its name a sense of great things, of things greater than yourself. A gracious, abiding, life-long influence! not merely the honour of your house, or the memory of your own intimate friends,—good and precious as these are,—but superadded to these, the love and reverence due to the common home, the generous mother of us all.

The last decade of the nineteenth century is passing away. The twentieth is approaching. It may seem a bold thing to say, but can we doubt that what its colour and tone will be in England depends in no slight degree on what those who are being brought up here, and in other public schools, shall become? We who are older may not hope to behold the working out of the momentous changes whose foreshadowing we already discern, and some of which we can hardly watch without awe. But *you*, by being true to your Christian belief, by your influence, by the part you take in the warfare of good against evil, *you* will have it in your power to mould the coming age. One cannot over-estimate the possibilities that hinge upon your boyhood.

Never to suffer the lamp of God to go out in the shrine of your hearts and your consciences,—never to forfeit your inheritance, or any of the vantage ground on which you stand, by indifference to or neglect or misuse of blessings won long ago for you laboriously by others, upon whose labours you have entered, but to be "a link among the days, to knit the generations each to each,"—let this be your aim and your resolve!

It is one thing to rest idly upon the achievements of our fathers; it is another to see in them the strongest call to fresh energy. It should be our aim "never to be forgetful of a truth once obtained from them, but never to sink into inertness in consequence of its attainment;"[1] or we may express the same duty thus: "Not to break with the past, but to put off the accretions of age." Does not that give us the proper mean between an unnecessary

[1] Mazzini.

idolatry of antiquity and a cutting ourselves adrift from it altogether?

To break with the past! Some there may be who are ready enough to do so—not afraid to slight all its monitory lessons—as there are some who with a light heart would make a *tabula rasa*, and treat as open questions everything hitherto regarded as most sacred. But which of us here would be among them? We cannot do so with the history of our school, or our nation, or our Christian religion. We cannot do so with our own individual lives. No! However much a man may chafe against the fetters of what he has been and what he has done,—however much he may try to laugh at old warnings of experience, however fondly he may fancy that he can start afresh any morning on a career of independence, still the solemn and sobering truth remains that "*God requireth*"[1] of each one of us—of you and of me—He requireth "*for judgment that which is past.*"

[1] Eccles. iii. 15.

Sermon XV.

THE VALUE OF INEQUALITY.[1]

"Unto every one that hath shall be given, and he shall have abundance: but from him that hath not, shall be taken away even that which he hath."—*Matthew*, xxv. 29.

OUR Saviour not rarely spoke in paradox —in unexpected and startling language, uttering words not to be pressed in the letter, but purposely put in such a form,—in order that his hearers might stir themselves to get at their inner and spiritual, their larger and deeper meaning.

This verse of my text is one of these rather hard sayings. Not that it drove people away. It is so, in a different way from that in which the discourse on the Bread of Life was hard. Then we read that many of the disciples said, "This is a hard saying, who can hear it?" and "many of them went back and walked no more with him."[2] But here there are no murmurs of dissent and disapproval. We are not told that any on this ground fell away

[1] Quinquagesima Sunday, February 28th, 1897.
[2] St. John, vi. 60, 66.

from Christ whenever the words were spoken. For they were repeated, and prominence is given to them. They were delivered on at least three different occasions, and very likely on others that have not been recorded.

This verse expresses, indeed, one of the profoundest laws of the moral world. We know that our Saviour often embodied parts of the best teaching of the past in His discourses. Transmuting them into the fine gold of perfect truth, he brought out of them more than had hitherto been detected within them. As He did not disdain to use such homely proverbial expressions as "Physician, heal thyself," "If the blind lead the blind, shall they not both fall into the ditch?" or, as when He gave the model of all prayer, He employed for some of its clauses what already existed in germ in Jewish forms of prayer,—so it may have been in this case.

"*To him that hath shall be given*" has the ring of a proverb applicable in its literal sense to the conditions of human prosperity. It was probably familiar to the shrewd worldly men of the time, like such sayings current among ourselves as "Money comes to money," "Nothing succeeds like success," "Fortune smiles on the fortunate." The words themselves were not novel. What was novel, and even startling (as has been remarked), was "that this principle should be adopted by Christ and laid down as one of those upon which God's government is carried on."[1] But we remember the parable in which the sharpness and quickness of the business-like steward forms the groundwork for the highest moral and spiritual teaching. And here, too, may we not say that something like that law of nothing succeeding like success may be traced in the conditions of growth in Christ-like, heavenly wisdom?

This aphorism, I said, we meet with at least three times; first, in St. Matthew's thirteenth chapter, when our Lord gave His reasons for speaking in parables; next, as the moral of the Parable of the Talents; and then again in that of the Parable of the Pounds, in St. Luke. The truth thrown out at first, to set the hearer thinking, was afterwards developed and expanded in those two longer passages.

"*Unto him that hath shall be given.*" I believe that one of the chief reasons why we find these words hard is because we will read into them our own narrow interpretation. We mistake their object; we do not grasp their fulness and their depth. We think of the opulent, the powerful, the influential, the

[1] Latham, "Pastor Pastorum," ch. x., to which I am indebted for the main thought, and for some expressions, in this sermon.

strong in physique, the robust in health, or persons constitutionally cheerful and buoyant; and so long as we limit the saying to such as are girt about with advantages of this sort, we must see in it little beyond a benediction upon the fortunate, and a curse, or something like a curse, pronounced on others who lack these gifts, and lack them through no fault of their own.

It is one thing to have a blessing, a grace or gift in the barest and most literal sense of having. It is another, and a very different thing to hold it, to appropriate it, to assimilate it. The very best and most nutritious food does not profit unless it be assimilated, converted into animal substance, so as to repair the daily waste of our bodily frames. If we see a young man started for life with a splendid equipment (ἀφορμή or χορηγία in Greek phrase), with all the advantages that can be supplied by birth and position, and freedom from all cares as to making his livelihood,— endowed with sufficient powers of body and mind—if we follow him after the seed-time of education is past, and then see him squandering all in a few years, throwing it all away through intemperance, or infatuation of one kind or another, or, if he does not come to that, sinking into a mere lounger and saunterer through life, can we say that he really has these blessings? He holds them by such a precarious tenure that, sooner or later, he will be parted from them. In the one case the laws of the moral government of the world will intervene; in the other, the spirit of our age will not tolerate him. There will be no room for the mere saunterer. The trifler and the idler are doomed. He has not acquired those advantages for himself. He has not earned them by toiling to improve them. He has not traded with his talents, whatever their original number, and made other two or other five besides them. To have endowments, in the highest sense of the word, we must feel their true value—and be alive to the importance—the necessity of cultivating what was bestowed.

> "For blessings which while they were ours
>   Alas! we knew not how to prize,
> Until they spread their snow-white wings,
>   And faded, faded from our eyes,
>   Forgive us, Lord, forgive!"[1]

This law of the using of blessings holds good, you know, in Nature. A muscle which is not exercised tends to degenerate. A limb that is used is strengthened; if disused, it becomes weak. And it penetrates the whole of a Christian's life.

[1] "Regrets" in "Fra Angelico and other Poems," y Dr. Gregory Smith.

If, then, we may say that to have, in its deeper sense, involves appreciating the possession, and using well the opportunities given do we not see what follows? We can understand how still more comes to the enlightened owner of a gift; how (as it has been tersely put) "the storing of achievement becomes the basis of additional achievement."[1] He alone who assimilates Christ's teaching can hope to receive continually more. If anyone is content to hear without appropriating and profiting—by and by he will obtain nothing, and at last even lose everything. It matters not whether we say he hath or he seemeth to have. For he who does not use (as Bengel says), "only seems to have."

The Bible will supply many an illustration of our text. The Apostles having some elements of spiritual wisdom, by using them rightly could pass on from strength to strength, from their earlier timid or faithless state, to the higher plane on which we find them moving in the Acts. So too, to take an example or two of those who had not, and from whom, therefore, was taken that which they had, the kingly power misused by Saul was transferred to David. The people of our Lord's day, even the rulers and teachers, with few or

---

[1] Canon Eyton, "The Search for God," Sermon II.

no sparks of true wisdom, and not using the little they had, were in danger of losing even that. The crowds upon the shores of the Lake of Galilee, after the feeding of the four thousand, forfeited what they had. They lost the presence of our Lord, when He left them and went to preach elsewhere. And so, to glance at the final lesson of Jewish History, the privileges that people had not known how to value, were "taken from them, and given to a nation bringing forth the fruits thereof."

But you may say, all this may be very true, but how does it clear up the inherent difficulty of the text? Your interpretation of it, by qualifying the meaning of its leading word "to have," does not altogether satisfy us. So read, the verse either becomes a truism, or remains a hard saying. Why choose a passage in which there still lingers an undertone of sadness? Yes, when we are in certain moods, almost of fatalism, and that haunts us ever and again with a feeling of perplexity? Why bring back to the mind what we would fain banish from it,—" the burden of the mystery, the heavy and the weary weight, of all this unintelligible world?"

Let me then ask you to consider this question of inequalities, and see if we cannot divest of its severity the sentence that sounds so terrible, "To him that hath shall be given ... from him that hath not shall be taken away even that which he hath."

God's world (let us first remember) is established and ordered on a basis not of equality, but of inequalities. It must, therefore, be right that they exist. It cannot be unjust; we should see it, if we could weigh all the equivalents in a just balance. It cannot be a curse, if we could regard it, as we may believe superior beings do, "with larger, other eyes than ours."

Look at one proof of it, in Nature, in vegetation, in the trees to whose "annual resurrection" we are beginning again to look forward, when

"all this leafless and uncolour'd scene
Shall flush into variety again."

"Each tree has (we are told) its own peculiar leaf-venation, corresponding to the peculiar arrangement of its own branches."[1] There is nothing like rigid equality or uniformity. The leaves of plants are variously modified, so as to suit their requirements. There is no end to their diversity of shape. Almost every species of plant has a different kind of leaf, adapted to the situation in which it grows, or to its general

[1] Hugh Macmillan, "Bible Teachings in Nature," ch. vii.; and see Sir John Lubbock's "Flowers, Fruits, and Leaves," ch. v.

structure and texture. And yet amidst all this diversity, nothing is capricious, nothing is accidental.

But further, take another thought about inequality, a far larger one, that of the great law of which vegetation is but one out of many examples. It has been shown in our time that it is out of *inequality* that all *progress* comes. "One little superiority gives an advantage for gaining a still greater superiority." " This orderly beautiful world is now and has always been the scene of incessant rivalry... From this stress of Nature, has followed the highest result we are capable of conceiving, continual advance towards higher and more perfect forms of life." "To it we owe all that is best and most perfect in life at the present day, as well as all its highest promise for the future."[1] Is it not striking to reflect that the law "*he that hath to him shall be given,*" is the law of individual excellence, the law by which "the world is so ordered as to favour the growth of one beginning to out-top the rest." Is it not, then, a miserable thing to dwarf our ideas of this subject to such a degree as to let it suggest nothing but the conditions of man's life on earth, and the differences between the fortunate

[1] Benjamin Kidd, "Social Evolution."

and the less favoured. Surely that is not all. It is but a portion, a section of the working out of God's law. Angels in this scene of inequality would discern a very different spectacle. We know but in part, as we are reminded in to-day's epistle, and as we require to be reminded again and again. It is a miserable thing to talk as Socialism does of redistributing and equalizing properties. I need not dwell on that. But one word may be allowed on capital, which the Socialist so hates. In this, too, is it not the use, not the mere possession, that is all important? "Capital," it has been said, "has no value at all, except when vivified by use."[1] Yes! *vivified* by use! Does not that expression help us to understand "He that hath to him shall be given, and he shall have abundance."

More, much more, might be added on the beneficial tendencies of this law of inequality. Oh, "how weary, stale, flat, and unprofitable" would this life become, did the opposite hold good! How monotonous the existence, how depressing the outlook, how great the paralysis to energy, if there were nothing else in store for our race but the dead level of uniformity, which, according to the forecast of some writers, is all that awaits it in the future.[2]

[1] Mallock, "Labour and the Popular Welfare."
[2] "National Life and Character," by C. H. Pearson.

St. Paul, at any rate, did not believe in any such dead level or monotonous drill. In the chapter[1] immediately preceding to-day's Epistle, he allows the widest play for individual character, for "diversities of gifts," yet with the same spirit working through them all. The best, the highest of these are to be earnestly desired, and carefully cultivated. Yet in the last verse, the link between the twelfth and thirteenth chapter, he says, "I show unto you a still more excellent way." Need I tell you in what that more excellent way consists? It is enshrined in those glowing words that describe Love, Charity, as it never before had been described. And believe that there is ample scope for its exercise here by you! How so? In recognizing, in accepting, in making the best of different types of character among yourselves, in loving and admiring what is above yourselves.

Thank God that the Christian character is not to be framed in any stereotyped or cast-iron mould. The largeness of Christ's teaching appears in nothing more than in the infinite variety of talents which He enlists in His service. Look at the Apostles. Each of them had a turn of mind that was specially his own. There was the thoughtful, contemplative John, there was the eager, practical,

---

[1] 1 Cor. xii.

impetuous Peter, and also the silent, reserved, yet honest and truthful Thomas. And so, may we not apply St. Paul's language and say: Are all to be great athletes? Are all to be eminent scholars? There is no reason why they should be. Let no tyranny of opinion, no rule of a narrow clique frighten any one of you from pursuing what he feels to be the true ideal for him. Let no cynical talk lower your high ambition, your ideal of becoming all you are capable of, and of turning your talent to the best possible account. There is an eternal, an essential distinctness in any character worth anything. It will never be merely a feeble repetition or imitation of another character. Let one who has physical strength, use it mercifully, value it, train it! Such training has braced many brought up here, to endure hardship as good soldiers of Christ, whether in some distant missionary field, or in the teeming populations of our English cities. He who has the gift of command and influence over others, let him study well how he employs that precious gift, not for private ends, but for the good of those who naturally look up to him as their leader. He who sets out with but a moderate equipment, but has the grace of perseverance, let him husband what he has, and go on steadily. Very likely he will hereafter distance some who may feel inclined to smile now at his humble efforts. Oh, how faulty are our predictions! That ideal hero of our times, Gordon, did not give very much promise at first of success in his profession. He had a delicate constitution which in later days hardened into iron. When at Woolwich, he was once told that he never would make an officer. His temper would blaze out fiercely in his younger days, but he gained the mastery over it. The roughest material is precious in the sight of its Maker and Fashioner. A sculptor was passing with a party of friends into his studio, when one of them, seeing a large, uncouth block, said, "*That* can never be turned to account." "Do not say so," was the reply, "I can see an angel in it."

Our Saviour, as we have seen, does not shrink from the consequences of inequalities. He prepares us for the fact that they widen, and more than this, that they are widened purposely. He implies that something like this holds good in all progress. It holds in Education. A clever boy, eager to learn, and asking intelligent questions, must forge ahead of the rest; he must get more attention, however conscientiously the teacher may distribute his pains. It holds in Religion. One who has no spark, or only the feeblest spark of desire for the things of the spirit, loses even the poor confusions he started with. While the trifler and indifferent find their powers first stagnate, and then dry up altogether, the earnest-minded grow and develop.

And it will hold, we may reverently believe, in that other state foreshadowed by the return of the Lord, in each of the two parables, the pounds and the talents. There is no hint of a dead level in that high world, in that home with the many mansions, where Christ said he would go to prepare a place for his followers, a place best fitted for each of them. What is the reward promised to the faithful servant, who has proved himself efficient in little things, or in a few matters? Is it something to be spent on his own gratification, a folding of the hands, a sitting down to a feast of selfish enjoyment? Very far from it! He is to have more authority, that is, more work, a wider range of duties, an ampler field for activity. A fresh and extended set of opportunities will be assigned to each individual and carefully graduated to every shade of character. More and more of the true riches is for those who have appreciated what they mean. More and more of the delight of being employed in God's service, in that kingdom where each shall humbly and thankfully accept the sphere appointed for him.

Such, or something like it, we may believe

to be the final goal, the Crown of Righteousness. But meanwhile, *life* with its responsibilities, and its priceless opportunities is yours. Looking on you, and forecasting what may be in store for you, who can help being penetrated with the thought of the momentous importance of this period of youth to you, the perilous choice it lays before you; the vital issues that it involves? True it is, on the one hand, that there is the mystery of the germs of evil springing up at a very early date—how subtle and secret in their origin, how frightfully rapid in their growth! But on the other hand, what glorious possibilities are yours! There is not one of you, who can have become so entangled in wrong-doing, as for the skein not to be unravelled betimes, and the clue to the right path recovered. Not one can there be upon whom the shades of the prison-house have already closed. The heaven that lay about your infancy is not yet very far off.

And what a prospect lies before you! We who have passed far beyond the middle arch of life, even if we are spared to witness the dawn of the next century, can hope to see but a very few pages of its book opened to us. But for you the bulk of that volume will be unfolded. The oldest among you may hope to live on to the middle of it. Grave questions, social, political, educational, religious, are coming to the birth, and you will have to take your part in solving them. They will vitally affect you, whatever be your rank, your wealth, or the past achievements of your fathers. The spirit of the coming generation will, we may be sure, require much more from those entrusted with much, than from others to whom less has been committed.

Suffer me then to say, as my last word, Learn your real self, and live up to it.[1] Follow after, cling to everything in this place that will foster it, and that can draw out your best, your highest powers. Remember those words of Bishop Butler:[2] "We are naturally trusted with ourselves; with our own conduct, and our own interest. We have temptations to be unfaithful to this trust, to forfeit this interest, to neglect it, to run ourselves into misery and ruin." Do not chafe at discipline. Believe that "it is good for a man that he bear the yoke in his youth." Have we not a convincing proof of its value, and at the same time a signal living example of the great law we have been considering,—the law of struggle rewarded, of talent cultivated bringing in an abundant return,—in the marvellous story of the great Norwegian explorer, Nansen, that is

[1] Cf. Pindar, "Pythian Odes," ii. 72, γένοι' οἷος ἐσσὶ μαθών.
[2] "Analogy," pt. i., ch. viii.

now in every mouth? How was he brought through difficulties, hardships, perils that might have made the stoutest heart quail? Was it not by having trained himself from youth to bear hardness? By deep study of the conditions of the problem before him? By unwearied attention to each minutest detail? Much he had indeed received to start with, but because he sedulously improved all his natural gifts, and never suffered one of them to rust, much more was added unto him.

Brave and temperate, cheerful, and patient, full of resource. What a lesson to our age is such a character as his! How it speaks to every ardent, enthusiastic spirit! How it seems to say to all: Do your very best! Never presume! Never despair! Never shrink from taking infinite pains!

> "Each in one thing excel the rest!
> Strive! and hold fast this truth of Heaven,
> To him that hath shall more be given!" [1]

---

[1] Robert Bridges, "Founder's Day."

BY THE SAME AUTHOR.

Crown 8vo, 7s. 6d.

TRANSLATIONS FROM PRUDENTIUS:
A SELECTION FROM HIS WORKS, RENDERED IN ENGLISH VERSE, WITH AN INTRODUCTION AND NOTES.

"It was a happy thought which led Mr. Thackeray to bring out a selection from Prudentius which gives the reader a fair idea of this little-known author within a reasonable compass. It is an edition which should satisfy all classes of readers."—*Athenæum*.

"We are very glad that Mr. Thackeray has taken in hand to make Prudentius accessible to more English readers than have previously known him. The selections are very well made, the translations (which are partly by Mr. Thackeray, and partly by friends of his) are, as a rule, both good and faithful, the scholarship of the introduction and notes is sound and unpretentious, and the get-up of the book very pretty."—*Saturday Review*.

"The Introduction is exceedingly interesting, with its account of Prudentius and its detailed exposition, likely to be useful to all students of Church history, of the light which Prudentius's poems throw on his age, on its social state and its religious practices."—*Guardian*.

Small crown 8vo, 7s. 6d.

MEMOIR OF
EDWARD CRAVEN HAWTREY, D.D.,
HEADMASTER AND AFTERWARDS PROVOST OF ETON.

With a Photogravure Portrait, a reproduction of Hawtrey's Bookplate, and 3 Coloured Illustrations from sketches by Mr. Francis Tarver, late French Master at Eton.

"The memoir is more in the nature of a sketch than of a complete life, but it is a sketch drawn with skill and care, and it leaves upon the mind a vivid impression of a remarkable character."—*Times*.

"There is quite enough here to enable the reader to form a true conception of Hawtrey."—*Athenæum*.

"Mr. Thackeray has done well with the scanty material put into his hands. He has given us a lively as well as a respectful portrait of the great headmaster."—*Journal of Education*.

"Mr. Thackeray's volume is full of interest."—*Spectator*.

Fcap. 8vo, 4s. 6d.

ANTHOLOGIA LATINA.
6TH EDITION, 1892.

Fcap. 8vo, 4s. 6d.

ANTHOLOGIA GRÆCA.
6TH EDITION, 1895.

LONDON: GEORGE BELL AND SONS.

www.ingramcontent.com/pod-product-compliance
Lightning Source LLC
Chambersburg PA
CBHW031817230426
43669CB00009B/1172